Jill Saudek was born in Oxford in 1946 and grew up in Marlow. She studied English literature at Newnham College, Cambridge University and became an English and drama teacher in a variety of schools. She retired in 2009 and now lives with her husband, son, daughter-in-law and three grandchildren in South East London. She has enjoyed reading her own stories and verses to all her small relatives but writing serious poetry is a new venture, undertaken during the covid lockdown.

To my ever-patient and loving husband.

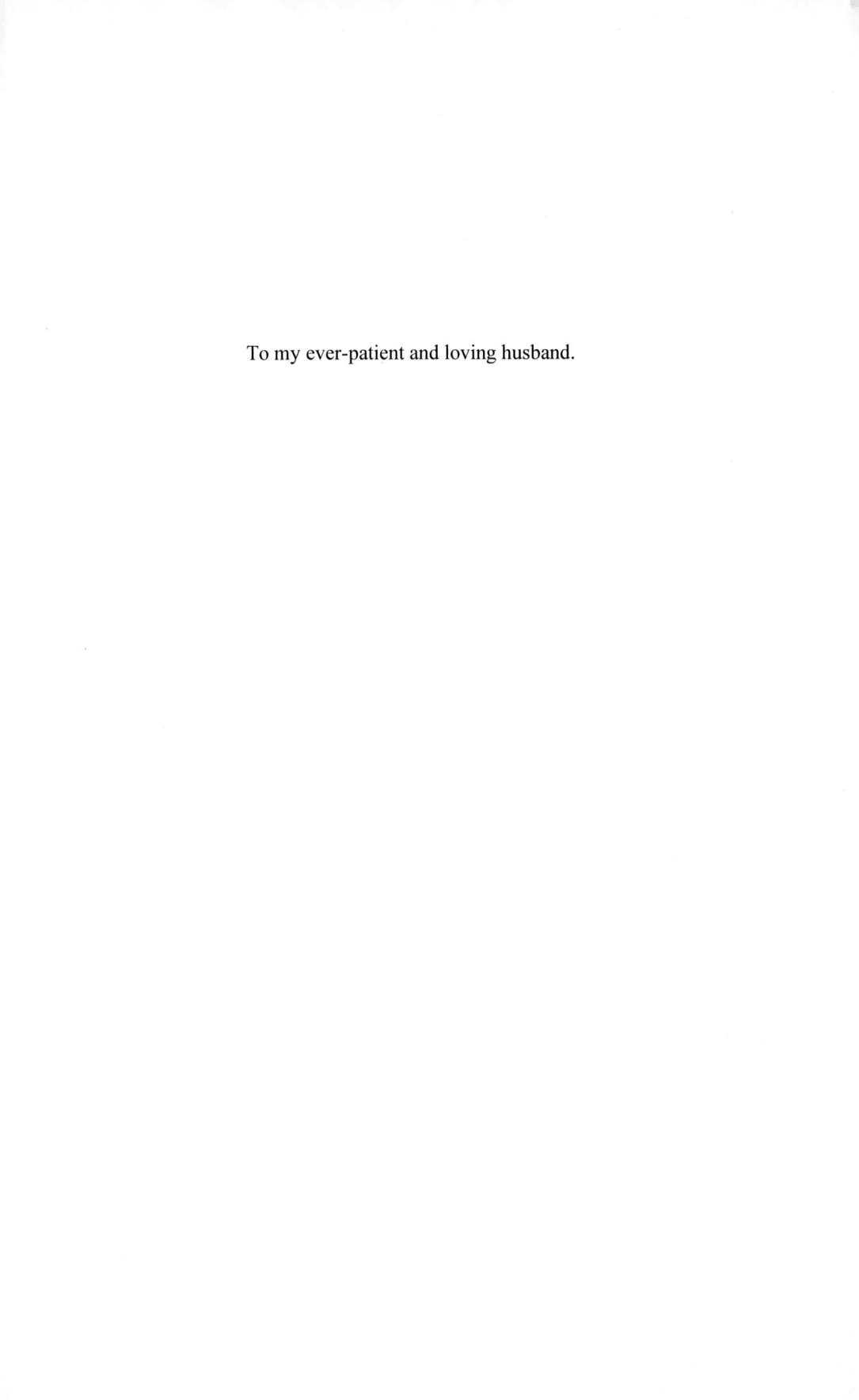

Jill Saudek

POEMS FROM PAINTINGS

AUSTIN MACAULEY PUBLISHERS™
LONDON * CAMBRIDGE * NEW YORK * SHARJAH

Copyright © Jill Saudek 2022

The right of Jill Saudek to be identified as author of this work has been asserted by the author in accordance with section 77 and 78 of the Copyright, Designs and Patents Act 1988.

All rights reserved. No part of this publication may be reproduced, stored in a retrieval system, or transmitted in any form or by any means, electronic, mechanical, photocopying, recording, or otherwise, without the prior permission of the publishers.

Any person who commits any unauthorised act in relation to this publication may be liable to criminal prosecution and civil claims for damages.

A CIP catalogue record for this title is available from the British Library.

ISBN 9781398459700 (Paperback)
ISBN 9781398459717 (ePub e-book)

www.austinmacauley.com

First Published 2022
Austin Macauley Publishers Ltd®
1 Canada Square
Canary Wharf
London
E14 5AA

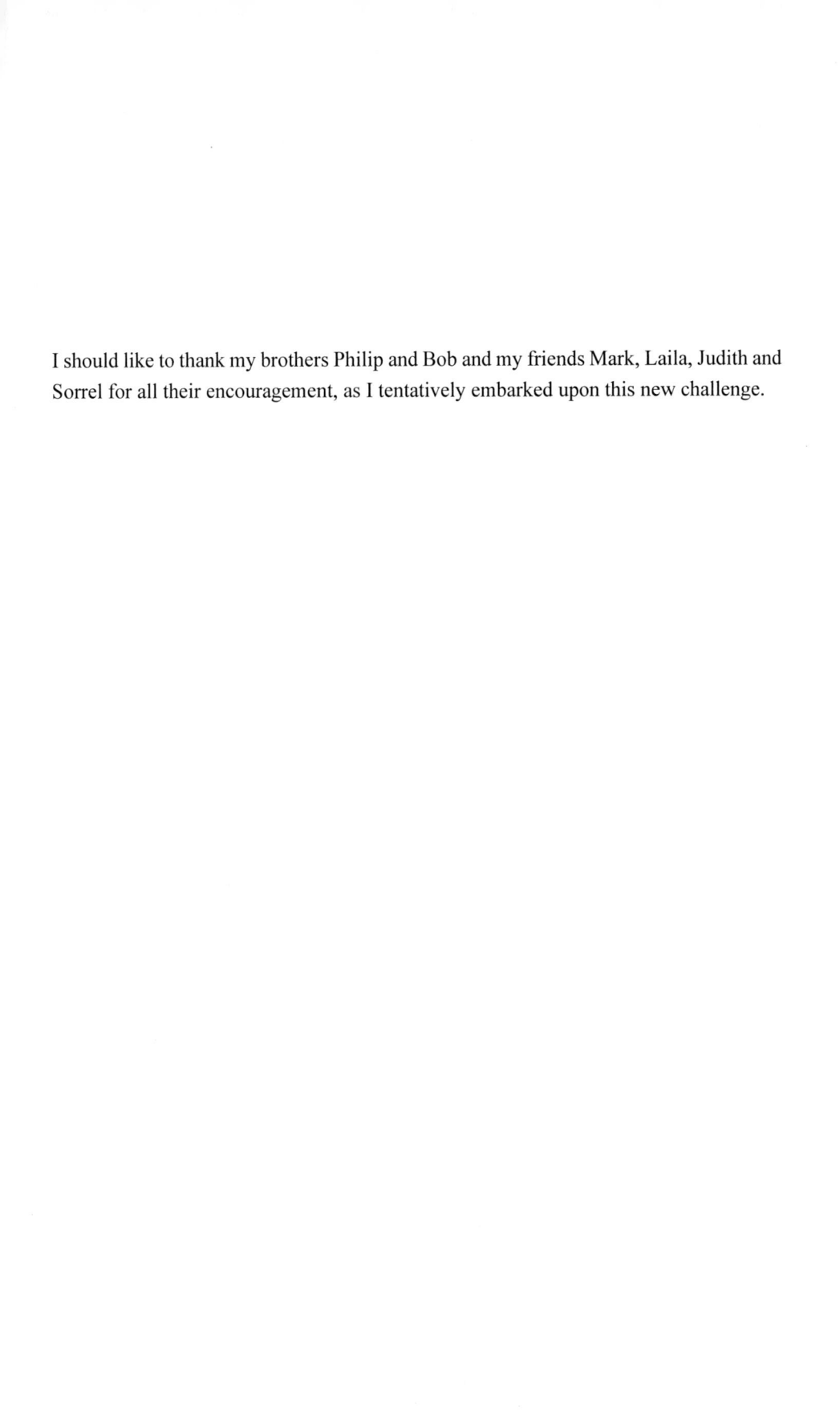

I should like to thank my brothers Philip and Bob and my friends Mark, Laila, Judith and Sorrel for all their encouragement, as I tentatively embarked upon this new challenge.

Table of contents

Introduction	15
Anon: The Book of Durrow – Matthew, C 700	16
Antonella Da Messina: Saint Jerome in His Study, 1474	18
Audubon Roseate Spoonbill – The Birds of America, 1835	20
Balla Giacomo: Flight of the Swallows, 1913	22
Giacomo Balla: Young Girl Running on a Balcony, 1912	24
Bassano: The Animals Entering the Ark, C 1575	25
Beardsley: Cover Design for Smithers' Catalogue of Rare Books, 1896	27
Blake: Pity, 1795	28
Boccione Umberto: States of Mind – Those Who Leave; Those Who Stay, 1911 Those Who Leave	30
Those Who Stay	31
Bonnard: The Open Window, 1921	32
Bosch: The Garden of Earthly Delights, C 1500	34
Botticelli: Primavera, C 1475	36
Ford Maddox Brown: The Last of England, 1855	38
Bruegel the Elder: Netherlandish Proverbs, 1559	40
Bruegel: Peasant Wedding Feast, 1567	43
Carpaccio: Two Venetian Ladies on a Balcony, 1475	45

Cezanne: Mont St Victoire, C 1905 — 47

Chagall: Above the Town, 1918 — 49

Chardin: The Governess, 1739 — 53

Constable: Flatford Mill, 1816 — 55

Lorenzo Costa: The Concert, C 1485 — 56

Walter Crane: The Horses of Neptune, 1910 — 58

Dali: The Hand Remorse, 1930 — 59

De Chirico: The Mystery and Melancholy of a Street, 1914 — 61

De Hooch: Woman and Child, 1665 — 63

Degas: Laundresses, 1884 — 64

Dürer: Melencolia 1514 — 66

Feininger: Schooner on the Baltic Sea, 1912 — 68

Ford Maddox Brown: Work, 1863 — 70

Fragonard: The Swing, 1767 — 73

Friedrich: Chalk Cliffs on Reügen (Faith, Hope and Charity), 1818 — 75

Friedrich: The Stages of Life, 1835 — 77

Gainsborough: Mr and Mrs Andrews, C 1750 — 78

Gaugin: Rupe Rupe, 1899 — 80

Mark Gertler: The Merry-Go-Round, 1916 — 82

Giorgione: The Sunset, 1506 — 83

Giorgione: The Tempest, C 1506 — 86

Gossaert: An Elderly Couple, C 1520 — 88

Goya: The Colossus, C 1808 — 90

Goya: The Third of May, 1808	92
Graf Urs: Young Woman and Hanged Man, 1525 (The Twa Corbies)	93
Grimshaw: Nightfall Down the Thames, 1880	95
Frans Hals: Portrait of a Young Man with a Skull, 1612	97
Hockney David: Garrowby Hill Yorkshire Wolds, 1998	98
Hogarth: An Election Entertainment, 1754	99
Hogarth: Marriage à la Mode 2 Tête-à-Tête, C 1745	101
Hopper: Nighthawks, 1942	103
Holman Hunt: The Scapegoat, 1855	105
Kandinsky Composition 8, 1923	106
Khnopff: An Abandoned City, 1904	109
Leonardo: Self-Portrait in Red Chalk (Aged About 60), 1510	111
Limbourg Brothers: The Book of Hours – Sign of Cancer, C 1414	113
Lowry: Coming from the Mill, 1930	115
Magritte: Pandora's Box, 1951	117
Magritte: The Lost Jockey, 1926	119
The Lost Jockey, 1942	121
The Lost Jockey, 1948	122
Manet: A Bar at the Folies Bèrgere, 1882	123
Master Bertram: God Creating the Animals Late 14 Century Master Bertram Contemplates the Sixth Day of Creation	125
Matisse: The Dessert (Harmony in Red), 1908	127
Millais: Autumn Leaves, 1856	129
Millet: Man Grafting a Tree, 1855	131

Monet: Autumn Effect at Argenteuil, 1873	133
Monet: A Field of Poppies, 1873	134
Monet: Path with Roses, Givenchy, 1902	135
Monet: Rouen Cathedral, 1890s	136
Monet: The Water Lily Pond with Japanese Bridge, 1899	138
Moreau Gustave: Oedipus and the Sphinx, 1864	139
Moreau Gustave: The Travelling Poet, 1891	141
Berthe Morisot: The Cradle, 1872	143
Munch: Moonlight, 1893	145
Munch: The Dead Mother and Child, C 1898	147
Nash: Dead Sea, 1940	148
Picasso: Girl Before a Mirror, 1932	150
Picasso: Weeping Woman	152
Piranesi: d' Invenzione stet Plate 15, 1751	154
Pompeii: Portrait of a Man and His Wife 79 AD (Seen in 1979 at the Royal Academy of Arts Exhibition)	156
Poussin: Dance to the Music of Time, C 1635	158
Poussin: Et in Arcadia Ego, 1637	161
Puvis de Chavannes: The Poor Fisherman, 1881	163
Raeburn: The Reverend Robert Walker Skating on Duddingston Loch, 1795	165
Odilon Redon: The Smiling Spider, 1881 A Cautionary Tale	167
Rembrandt: Self-Portrait with Two Circles, C 1665	169
Renoir: At the Theatre – La Première Sortie, 1876	171

Renoir: Picking Flowers (In the Field), C 1890	173
Rousseau: Tiger in a Tropical Storm, 1891	175
Rubens: Peace and War, 1630	176
Schiele: Sunflower, 1917	178
Schwabe: The Angel of Death, C 1898	180
Seurat: La Grande Jette stet, 1884	181
Spencer: The Resurrection Cookham, 1924	183
Steenwyck stet: The Vanities of Human Life, C 1640	184
Steinlen Théophilé Alexandre: Gust of Wind and Pastoral Scene, 1905	186
Stubbs: Horse Attacked by a Lion, 1769	188
Tanning Dorothea: A Little Night Music, 1943	190
Titian: Bacchus and Ariadne, 1523	192
Turner: Hannibal Crossing the Alps, 1812	194
Turner: Norham Castle Sunrise, C 1845	196
Turner: Rain, Steam and Speed, the Great Western Railway, C 1844	197
Turner: Snowstorm at Sea, 1842	199
Uccello: The Battle of San Romano, 1432	201
Van Gogh: Wheatfield with Sower, 1888	202
Van Gogh: The Sower, 1888	203
Van Gogh: Almond Blossom, February, 1890	204
Van Gogh: Les Alycamps (Autumn), 1888	206
Van Gogh: The Bedroom at Arles, C 1889	207
Van Gogh: The Potato Eaters, 1885	209

Van Ruisdale: An Extensive Landscape with a Ruined Castle and a Village Church, C 1665	**211**
Velasquez: The Water Seller of Seville, C 1620	**214**
Velasquez: Las Meninas, 1656	**216**
Vermeer: Lady Writing a Letter with Her Maid, 1670	**218**
Vermeer: The Artist's Studio, 1666	**221**
Warhol: Diptych, 1962	**222**
Watteau: Journey to Cythera, 1717	**224**
Whistler: Nocturne in Black and Gold – The Falling Rocket, C 1872	**225**
Wright: The Experiment with the Air Pump, 1768	**226**
Wyeth: Christina's World, 1948	**230**

Introduction

Writing these poems meant that I spent much more time really looking at the paintings, in a way I had not done before. Most of the artists are well-known but I also discovered a number of whom I had not previously heard. I used various books of reproductions, although it was, of course, wonderful to view just a few of the original paintings in all their intensity: for example, I remember seeing Turner's poor hare menaced by the approaching steam train, a crucial detail which is often dimmed in reproduction. My hope is that the reader would also be encouraged to ponder the paintings (all readily available on the Internet) in depth, preferably before reading the poems. I have no academic knowledge of the visual arts and my approach is entirely subjective – thus the reader may well disagree with my interpretations, although, I always tried to capture the spirit of each painting, as I saw it.

Anon: The Book of Durrow – Matthew, C 700

I read that this is from the seventh century –
An early inspiration for my poetry!
Why did it catch my eye? What does it mean to me,
Here at my laptop in secular twenty-twenty?
I know the Bible texts but have lost my simple faith,
Believing in the bleak finality of death,
Though when I sing in church, I listen to the Gospels,
And when I leave, the sound of pealing bells,
The sight of soaring steeple still move me
With a sense of the transcendent. Yet this picture
Shows a vulnerable, uncertain figure –
Matthew, whose apostolic symbol is mere man.
His eyes meet mine, from the far Saxon past,
Across time's unimaginable span
Perhaps still searching, or perhaps still lost
In the maze of what his great encounter meant:
Could it be true that the Man was heaven-sent?
His downturned, half-closed mouth signals confusion,
As if he doubts the improbable conclusion
Drawn from what he witnessed. His small, awkward feet
Make him look ungainly, while his arms and hands
Hang helpless, caught within the heavy weight
Of the bell-shaped cape. Does he understand
The perfect, chequered absolutes, which he must bear
Now that he has been made into a monument
To represent Christendom, always, everywhere?

A small illuminated egg, a pearl of light,
Is lying, perhaps unnoticed, at his feet;
Is this what the old monastic artist meant –
That it would hatch beyond the apostle's knowing,
Time-travelling and timeless truth bestowing?
The curling, interwoven, patterned spirals
Surely proclaim a heavenly interpretation,
As symmetry, beauty overwhelm denial
Of God's great purpose, his divine intention;
And yet, to me, that puzzled, human expression
Speaks of man's everlasting doubt and hesitation.

Antonella Da Messina: Saint Jerome in His Study, 1474

Immersed in his own thoughts, stern-faced, he reads,
And it is as if we see into his mind –
The wooden cell that guards his privacy;
For inside here is everything he needs;
No longer will he travel far to find
His truth; God's undiscovered country
Has been explored, is much-loved and familiar –
His long, eventful journey's promised end;
The soaring arches of the fine cathedral
Reach beyond his vision into a space
Already filled within the vast interior
Of his meditation. The sunlit background
The soaring of wild birds beyond the window,
Mean nothing to this dedicated cardinal
Who contemplates infinity in this small place.
He has found light, while much else stays in shadow;
Movement, as he sits motionless and still,
The peacefulness that comes with certainty,
And, as he turns the pages of the Bible,
He sees the illumination of eternity.
Outside, upon the marble windowsill
The peacock and the partridge stand immobile,
With richly patterned tails and wings, tight-furled,
Seeming to spurn the joyful gift of flight;
Heraldic images, denying their true nature,
Renouncing the inheritance of living creature,

Reflecting the Saint's precious inner light,
They mimic the static vision of his world.
Only the faithful lion, his front paw raised,
Longs to roam the desert whence he came,
And break free from the bounds of prayer and praise
To a distant God without a name.
He longs to feel and smell the ground beneath
His pounding feet; the tiles are hard and cold,
Their decorated beauty meaningless;
Once he was wild, adventurous and bold –
Loving to feel the wind, to take deep breaths
Of mountain air; yet, despite his distress,
He remains loyal to the gentle human
Who once, so long ago, healed his sore pain,
Removed the thorn that had imprisoned him
Gave him the precious power to move again.
But even stronger than his fierce desire
For freedom to roam again his wilderness,
To feel on his gold mane the sun's hot fire,
Is his perception of his Master's loneliness.
And thus, with faithfulness, with love and gratitude
Lion and man embrace their servitude.

Audubon Roseate Spoonbill – The Birds of America, 1835

I imagine the extraordinary patience
With which the artist studies the glorious bird,
Keeping such a reverential silence
That even his quiet breath will not be heard.
His subject, like himself, is poised and balanced,
So that the clear blue waters are not stirred
And the little fish will near the surface,
Unwary, eyes by dazzling sunlight blurred.
The spoonbill's eye shines brightly as he waits
His time to enter the water from the shore;
The artist's eyes widen in wonder as he creates
An image that will last for ever more,
Memorialising Nature's fine designs,
The great abundance of God's generous spirit –
While Man with his meticulous drawn lines
Can mimic creation through his skill and merit –
Such power lies within the artist's hand!
But now, a darker shadow sweeps the land –
Knowledge taints innocent appreciation,
I look again and now I understand
The cruelty of Audubon's great conception.
Firstly, he shoots his prey then lugs it home,
Arranges its body on taut wires and strings
So that a faithful portrait may be drawn
Of those soft-feathered, gently lifted wings.
Then he is done, another page completed

To satisfy his wild, lifelong obsession –
The process will be patiently repeated
To achieve his great classification.
Lifesize, the still-life birds in moving pose,
Still warm, hang lifeless his aim to fulfil –
He had caused their beating wings' death throes,
Then given them life again, for ever still.
Perhaps he mused that God would wish it thus –
All living creatures know no other way,
Are driven onward by no other purpose
Than to watch and wait – and then live off their prey.

Balla Giacomo: Flight of the Swallows, 1913

O swallow, swallow, flying, flying south (Tennyson)

Through the waning sunlight, in and out of shadows
Fly the swallows –
They know warm days will cease and winter come,
So they leave home;
In north countries, the brief blue glimpse of sky
Deceives: Time will, as they must, fly –
Therefore they, restless, leave
Their summer lodgings under homely eaves.
In the swirl and curve of flight
They'll trace their path by white magnetic light,
Before they roost at fall of night.
Now in ordered harmony they follow
Their brave leader; O swallow, swallow,
Your lovely symmetry
Of gently arching, outstretched wings,
Mirrored in miniature forked tails,
Enables you to make that epic journey
Beyond human imaginings,
Over strange seas where glimpses of great whales
Leap high above a heaving ocean,
Echoing your awe-inspiring motion.
Finally, you return to last year's sun-baked nest
And take your rest.
We order our lives so that we stay safe,

Protected from the icy winter's wrath,
Sheltered from the north wind's fearsome blast
In geometric structures that will last:
Right-angled, straight-lined is our symmetry,
We build in wood and glass, robust and heavy;
We cannot share your daring, winged fluidity
But cling to our secure, static rigidity.

Giacomo Balla: Young Girl Running on a Balcony, 1912

She is fire and air
Sun and sky
There she goes
Tip-toes
Heels
A streak, a glance
Of shimmering light
She feels
The pulsing dance
The iron-barred balcony
Barely seen
Fades into green
She takes flight
This running girl
With red-gold hair
Her full skirt's swirl
A particle's whirl
Always in motion
Joyous explosion
Formless
Breathless
Timeless.

Bassano: The Animals Entering the Ark, C 1575

All is harmonious here – no haste or urgency
Despite the tumultuous chaos that God's plan
Will soon unleash – the terrible destruction
Of living creatures – animals, birds, man.
Rain will pour down from a wrathful heaven,
The land will drown under a surging sea;
Yet Noah lifts his hand in benediction –
He has embraced this precious chance to save
The whole world from the horror of extinction
Beneath the darkness of a mountainous wave.
The humans gladly accept, it seems, their role
In preparation for the mighty task –
They have seen corruption of the soul
And they will do whatever their God will ask
Obediently, without demur or question,
Seeing the justice of His punishment –
We see the quiet calm of their expression
As they fulfil the orders He has sent.
The artist also lets us see a miracle:
Nature transfigured, for the divine spark
Of reason has entered every animal
Chosen from countless hordes to board the ark.
As if directed by some heavenly angel
To understand and to accept their fate,
The beasts have made their way to this one place
Of sanctuary – patiently, they wait

Their turn, filled with a blessed grace.
Two by two, up the great ramp together
Leaving the wildness of their former lives,
Ruthless combat dissolved in a new order
Where no one kills to live, yet all survive.
The faithful donkey humbly bears his burden,
The dogs and cats are peacefully at play
In this new world: here is another Eden,
As at the golden dawn of the sixth day.
Forty days of storm and flood will come,
The little ark will tremble on the void
Until God's need for vengeance has destroyed
All the last traces of their former home.
Not until the land has been washed clean
Of disobedience to His holy law
May man and bird and beast come forth again…
And all will be just as it was before.

Beardsley: Cover Design for Smithers' Catalogue of Rare Books, 1896

Constrained by the closed, drawn, blinded window,
Enchained like the exotic bird inside,
Cornered by heavy bars on the striped sofa,
She reads, now freed to wander far and wide;
The ground beneath her feet, a rippling river
On which she floats, upheld by spreading gown –
Her lips part in amazement, as a shiver
Of expelled breath loosens her tight-laced bodice
And her luxuriant hair soft-tumbles down;
She who was so innocent, chaste and modest –
Respected, as a dowry-bearing daughter,
Feels her breasts swelling with new-born desire;
In her soft hand the book is turned to water,
Her chaste cheeks burn, her nostrils breathe fierce fire;
Her hat, a burgeoning garden of sweet flowers
Thrusts upward, overwhelms her wondering brain –
She reads the rare book in a new-born era:
My lovely Lady will never be her former self again.

Blake: Pity, 1795

Macbeth:
And Pity, like a naked new-born babe
Striding the blast, or heaven's cherubim horsed
Upon the sightless couriers of the air
The Merchant of Venice:
The quality of mercy is not strained,
It droppeth as the gentle rain from heaven
It is twice blessed

To leave the headlong rush across the sky,
To turn another way, drawn by the misery
Of all who lie helpless, hands clasped in dumb prayer,
To feel, imagine, see with the mind's eye
Through the darkening clouds that sweep the air,
Across the estranging gulf – this is true pity.
The new-born babe leaps joyful, arms spread wide,
Fearless despite the storm's tumultuous blast –
Fount of forgiveness, innocently given
To those whose upcast eyes could find no heaven,
But stared sightless as the cherubim passed
Beyond, and their unspoken hopes denied.
The horses fly so swiftly on the wind,
Oblivious to the troubled earth below,
To all the suffering of humankind;
But now the gentle rain falls soft and low
And merges with the tears of grief that flow
From the deep wells of an anguished mind.
And then may Pity's power flood the world,

Drown the harsh winds, temper the fierce force
Of the pale horses' path, slow their wild course,
And bathe with insight their unseeing eyes,
So that a new-born vision may arise,
And the twice-blessed Mercy be unfurled.

Boccione Umberto: States of Mind – Those Who Leave; Those Who Stay, 1911 Those Who Leave

Grimly, he peers out of the train window
Which cruelly reflects his anguished face;
Fragments of his past fade into shadow,
All is in flux, nothing can hold its place;
Tall houses gape, open-mouthed in horror,
Trees bend in anguish as he rushes past,
Distorted by the whirlwind's icy blast,
Lone witnesses to his enforced departure.
Helpless, he's carried towards an unknown future,
As half-glimpsed ghosts leer in mocking scorn,
Masked with hideous, barely human feature,
Then vanish as he journeys on, alone,
Heading towards a meaningless new dawn,
Drowning in the swirl of wind and water,
Bereft of all that had once been familiar –
How can he fight for what he loves when all that he loves has gone?

Those Who Stay

They went to the station,
Saw the train depart
Without them;
They drift in confusion,
Cold in their heart,
Defeated in soul,
Lost in mind,
Self-condemned,
Grey, spectral,
Wrapped in shrouds,
Drifting clouds
In a bitter wind,
Unreal.
There was a call
That they would not hear,
An appeal
Shunned through fear.
The green rods of cowardice
Beat on their bent backs, ice
Dagger, spear
Of an unforgiving storm,
As they slink home.

Bonnard: The Open Window, 1921

The drowsy heat of afternoon…
The blind should be drawn shut
Making a shadowy cocoon
To keep the fierce sun out,
And let the soft red, sheltering room
Resemble an enclosing womb;
But here is an open window
Inside her spellbound mind –
She sleeps upon ethereal blue sky
Soaring high
On a strengthening wind;
Pillowed by one soft hand, she dreams
Of flying over billowing trees to follow
The dazzling golden gleams,
Loosed arrows
Of desire that promise her so much,
Shining through the hard glass pane
Turning the curtain into golden rain
Wakening the furled buds with sweet smell,
Releasing them from their containing jar
With burning, yearning fire.
She dreams of a gentle touch
On her soft curve and swell,
On the deep cleft under the dark-leaved wood
Of her impending womanhood.
The playful kitten lifts its paw in vain –

She will not now return
To innocent, childish things
Her imaginings
Take her afar,
For she must soon explore the green foothill,
Ascend the rocky crag, and climb
The mountain. She knows that it's time,
That there will be no standing still.
Now the mosquitoes' whine,
The cicadas' incessant knock
Unfasten the dark cupboard's glittering lock
And let her shine.

Bosch: The Garden of Earthly Delights, C 1500

In that breathless moment before time began,
When the first breath of wonder was indrawn by man
On seeing the pure beauty of the woman,
Even there, even then,
The stuff of living was born out of contrast,
Ecstasy
Sprung from variety,
The spin and quiver and turn
That do not last.
For Bosch, the everlasting fire is lust –
The pitiless flames of Hell that burn
On the last panel of this fantastic,
Terrifying triptych.
In Eden, contrasts seem, at first, restrained:
The lucent white of man and unicorn,
Elephant and giraffe, swan and heron –
With muted hues of gentle blue and green
That permeate the quietness of the scene.
But look more closely at this lovely land:
The dark background of twisted, rocky mountains,
The elaborate elegance of the wrought rose-fountain
Serve to enhance the stillness and awed silence
Of that first held breath; for the fountain flows;
Its plash, the drumming of the wind that blows
Across the wild, grey, unexplored distance
Both rupture and intensify the central peace;

The movement of wispy, windblown clouds on high
The spiralling flocks of birds that freely fly
Dancing, circling in unbounded sky
Show life is change, motion that does not cease.
Now hear the screams and roars of primal struggle,
Lives lost and won in necessary battle:
The rat in the cat's maw, the lion's growl
As it devours the deer, the birds' harsh squawks
As they hold helpless, dangling in their beaks
The lower reptiles; the frogs' frenzied croak,
The grunt and oink that sow and litter make
As they pursue their prey. All this, the crouching owl
Knows, in his wisdom. What salvation
For these birds and beasts of God's creation?
At the heart of all art, all imagination,
Lies contrast: the tortured throes, the agony
Of the damned, the promise of redemption;
And everywhere in well-shaped, composed form,
Moving within the moment held in time,
We see how contrast brings intensity:
The innocent wonder of that indrawn breath
Intertwined, like the snake's coil round the Tree,
With knowledge of love and lust, of life and death.

Botticelli: Primavera, C 1475

The garden of eternal spring in May
Where love's Goddess, the immortal Venus,
Haloed by foliage, lifts her hand to bless
All those who follow her harmonious way:
In circling dance, the nymphs bestow their grace,
Flora strews flowers on the soft green grass
Blossom and fruit embroider orange trees,
And all is lovely in this hallowed place,
For spring has come. But how long can it stay?
Framing the centre, where all serves to sweeten,
Time past and future this frail present threaten,
For when spring comes, then winter is on its way.
Mercury lifts his weapon, the snaky caduceus,
Endeavouring to keep the clouds at bay
Which seek to darken this quiet sunlit day;
Then night's prowling predators roam loose
Intent on prey, inflicting deadly harm;
His sheathed sword must surely soon be drawn –
Watchful, he stands erect, as if to warn
The innocent spirits that danger will come.
Venus' own son strings his playful bow –
The blind boy will not let things rest in peace,
For innocence must pass, content must cease,
So he lets loose his burning, flame-tipped arrow.
Zephryus, the wild wind from the west
With cold grey wings and icy, billowing cape
Overwhelms Chloris; she struggles to escape,
In vain, the powerful blast of pitiless lust;

But see the transformation! Former horror
Now a memory; her swelling curves, her smile –
Her fingers touch the seat of love, beguile
All the sad past: she is the radiant Flora,
Beautiful in body, joyful in her mind.
Ah – *if Winter comes, can Spring be far behind?*

Ford Maddox Brown: The Last of England, 1855

A fierce wind and a stormy sea –
My grim determination
To choose a different destiny
To cross a mighty ocean.

I must do as I am bid
For better or for worse –
I try to keep my fears well-hid –
I have no other choice.

You should not turn to gaze behind
To see what lies to leeward;
Banish home thoughts from your mind
And look ahead, look seaward.

He will not let me bid farewell,
He will not tell me why;
He holds me in the heaving swell
As I stifle my cry.

The past is past – it's done, it's over –
And you must needs look forward –
There's only one way to recover,
I know you are no coward.

Ah, but I am the fitful sail,
I veer, tremble and quiver –
The sharp teeth of the icy gale
Make me quake and shiver,
Bring into my eyes hot tears –
I dare not raise my hand
To wipe the sorrow of past years –
He will not understand.

I take her gloved hand in my own,
I try to comfort her:
We cannot do this on our own
For we are bound together.

Ill-omened crow, the black umbrella
Which he holds over me –
Cannot protect from stormy weather
Nor from the vast sea.

I have my books, my strength, my health,
My indomitable spirit;
I go to find adventure, wealth,
And she must learn to bear it.

"O husband, husband, take me home –
The land is close, look there!"
But such poor words will never come,
From my silent despair.

We leave cold, gloom and poverty
Behind, as we are hurled,
Onward to opportunity,
Of a brave, new world.

Bruegel the Elder: Netherlandish Proverbs, 1559

"The number of fools is infinite…"
Here, in the hands of Bruegel, what delight
It gives the viewer to observe the folly
Of countless men and women, who are wholly
Engrossed, while also being unaware!
Look there – and there – and there – and over there –
So much ardent, single-minded energy
Is being expended on stupidity
That you could easily spend days just gazing
In wry recognition of the amazing
Idiocy of others – rather like ourselves?
See the glum farmer who scrupulously delves
To bury the water underneath the earth
After the calf has fallen to his death;
Nearby, observe the crafty, black-clad fool
Finding much ado and not much wool,
Shearing a pig. And then, talking of swine,
Look at the elegant blue cap – very fine –
Atop its owner, who thinks he is so wise
To cast roses before their porcine eyes.
Why let the bristly boar drink from the barrel?
Herein there must lie many a sobering moral,
For example, act Decisively:
The woman with fire and water cannot see
The way to escape the chaos all around;
With a decisive bump on the hard ground,

Falls the witless, dithering fool
Who tried in vain to sit between two stools!
But if you want to take careful precaution,
Thinking your way through each potential option,
Then copy the cat owner, armed to the teeth
Lest his old moggy should escape beneath
The rerebrace he wears to shield his arm,
Which with its teeth will do him mortal harm.
Banging your head against a thick brick wall
Will not improve your reasoning power at all –
Signs of intelligence are in short supply –
But worse yet is the calculated lie.
For Bruegel also illustrates deceit:
Witness the cunning, defecating cheat
Who fiddles with the pack of cards and throws
Away the key ones, under the nose
Of the unwitting players in the throes
Of argument, leading each other by the nose!
The young wife oh so cunningly deceives
Her aged husband who, poor fool, believes
The blue cloak shows she cares for his fragility;
How she exploits his imbecility!
Her touch is hardly gentle, gives no comfort –
For she has both the guile and will to thwart
Any investigation of adultery –
But shouldn't count on the complicity
Of the old gossips who, above all, love prying
On the young and pretty. Also spying
On intimate relations is the spurned lover
Who may yet wield his sharp knife and discover
Her secret, to the joy of the sanctimonious.
In contrast, optimistic rather than odious,
The young man shoots his feathered arrows high
Aiming to catch elusive pies in the sky.
I could go on and on, but my crude rhyme
Is hardly worthy of your precious time;

Go, contemplate the painting, for instruction
And entertainment. You will find the construction
Quite wonderful – the sheer finesse and beauty
With which the artist illustrates one's duty,
The vivid colours of each separate character,
Their poise and pose, through which you can infer
A none-too-serious expression of the moral,
And see the wisdom in every proverbial fable!
With his brushstrokes, the master is proving
The unexamined life is not worth living!

Know thyself, the old philosopher advised –
But here, it is Art that's the more richly prized:
If acts purely of probity and wisdom had been done
Then where would be the inventiveness and where the fun?

Bruegel: Peasant Wedding Feast, 1567

I have never *seen* such noise before,
Nor simple food enjoyed with so much relish!
Even the bagpipes' overwhelming roar,
The reedy grumblings of the bass bassoon
Barely penetrate the raucous din –
The players play on, while all the rest replenish
Earthenware cup, bread platter, wooden bowl,
One hungry peasant calling out for more –
More here, he thinks, than he has seen all year.
It seems that nearly everyone in the parish
Has been invited and is feasting here.
At the far end the greedy peasants sprawl,
And bawl, adding to the caterwaul.
The musicians must wait before they can begin,
They eye the greedy guests with growing fear
What if this plenty were to disappear?
In the centre sits the bride, her whole
Being far removed from the great clamour –
Eyes closed, hands clasped in meditative prayer,
She is rapt in contemplation of her soul,
Hoping that this night all may be well.
She's not the only one to ignore the fare:
At the head of the table sits the local mayor –
His wolfhound, symbol of his brutal power,
At his feet, feeding on the brown crumbs
Fallen from a savoury, soft white roll.

Will he be claiming his *droit de seigneur*?
He's deep in discourse with a holy nun –
Can she persuade him to forego his cruel
Right, which any pious man should shun?
Will he release the bride from this night's peril –
For what is done can never be undone.
In the foreground sits a little girl,
Wrapped warmly, for her nose is red and raw,
Stuffing herself in frantic haste, pell-mell –
She isn't used to this sublime splendour,
Which may soon vanish under a fairy's spell!
The room is lit with reds and green, their colour
Mingling with the golden floor and wall,
Creating a wonderful, dizzying swirl.
Her bonnet has a precious peacock feather
She wants to show it off, but not until
She has finally appeased her hunger,
Only when she has devoured her fill.
Before her pass the red-capped, sprightly waiters,
She hears the stamp and tramp of booted leather,
Responding to the rhythm's dancing call.
This is the greatest night in the whole calendar –
Nothing could ever be so magical!
Will the clock chime for her, like Cinderella
Expelled before the end of the Prince's ball?
Will she soon be driven to surrender
To the everyday, the humdrum, after all?
For every guest has hard work to be done:
Muffled by music, comes the faint, far call
Of fields in waiting, once the busy sun
Has wakened them to a new day of labour
So that the wheat they've planted may grow tall,
Before the winter comes and cold nights fall.

Carpaccio: Two Venetian Ladies on a Balcony, 1475

O but this is wearisome –
The everlasting tedium
Of each interminable day;
Even the dogs won't play,
The birds won't fly away
But squat, too fat
And indolent to take the torpid air.
The women's neatly coiffured hair
Stays in place, as they also must do,
Staring sightless at the familiar view;
They are past their prime –
Their gorgeous glory-time
Has been long gone,
And now they sit alone
Trapped in their palatial home,
Where admirers can no longer come.
Emptied of spirit, lackadaisical;
The one surviving sparkle
Is in the costly jewellery
Above each drooping bosom,
Hanging heavy as a manacle.
With gesture mechanical,
One lady thrusts the stick
At the crouching dog; stuck
Fast, the two of them – no walk
Allowed for him nor her, no talk

Of what had been her former life
When she had been a woman, not a wife
And loved to stand and see
The view from her grand balcony,
When she was once on view
And people saw her too.
The page boy reaches to caress
The chained bird; she can only guess,
Now, how lovely that must feel,
Chained as she is too in this unreal,
Beautiful fair city,
Hardly sitting pretty,
Out of her mind with boredom
And all the long, long life to come.

Cezanne: Mont St Victoire, C 1905

Man's harmony with nature in the foreground –
Sun-drenched fields of vivid green and gold;
Planted hedgerows, all in well-planned order
Delineate and contain the land around;
Generations of proud farmers, young and old
Protect their riches within linear border
And pass these family treasures to their children;
Since Adam, men had dug, had dug and delved,
Turning, through their dedicated toil,
The wilderness into a pleasant garden,
And in the labour they'd defined themselves
And brought forth plenty from the fertile soil.
Small buildings show where they have taken root –
They live like kings within their promised land,
Humble, illiterate farmers who have striven,
Indifferent to fame or fortune, mute,
Content, with aching back and soiled hands,
To tend what God and bounteous nature had given.
The many arches of the fine stone bridge
Symbolise a different human instinct:
To travel freely, venture forth elsewhere –
Perhaps across the darkly shadowed ridge
Beyond the reach of home, though always linked
To home by countless centuries, before
The urge to see another world took hold
And they abandoned their birth-right of old.
The wind in the trees,
Evergreen leaves

In lullaby caressed
Their childish dreams,
Whispering no change;
But sunrise gleams
Disturbed their rest –
Birds flying to strange
Countries over perilous seas
By fierce storms blown,
Made them pine for wider range,
To leave ancestral lands, to seize
The lure of the unknown…
And always, in the distance, the great mountain reared
Its stubborn, rocky head – and an imagined world,
Masked by its peak, of other countries far beyond,
Mocked their ignorance; lightning flashes seared
The open skies, and seedlings stirred, unfurled
And grew inside their minds, to bid a fond
Farewell – and to fare forward, seeking new adventures
Outside the Eden of their safe, familiar pastures,
To cast aside the chains of ponderous history,
To find beyond the horizon a new story.

Chagall: Above the Town, 1918

Once upon a time, two lovers met
In the quaintest little town
Nestling sweetly, snugly, down
Beneath a sloping mountainside;
Their meeting was a dark secret;
Something they would have to hide,
On fearful peril of their lives,
Because, beneath the surface charm
Of painted houses, model farm,
There flashed deadly knives:
Spite, from ancient grudge, would harm
Lovers who came from different sides.
The tale has been told before –
When bitter families at war
Have clipped the wings of fledglings, caught
In tangled snares of angry thought.
Ah, best-beloved little children,
Such a dreadful, heavy burden
Should not be for you to shoulder;
But you must hear my narrative
And then, perhaps, when you are older,
You may too escape alive.
This little town was shut off quite,
By jagged fences; day and night
While the people worked or slept
The local armed militia kept
Keen watch, to check on who would leave,
Who, reckless, might try to deceive;

Thus, all entrances were barred
And no one could evade the guard –
Who carefully the papers checked
Of all they deemed to be suspect –
For one half of the population
Suffered trial and tribulation,
Were shunned, despised, never allowed
To meet the rest who, cruel, proud,
Kept themselves aloof, apart.
But what, you ask me, of the heart?
Can you extinguish burning love
By proclamation from above?
Impossible, methinks, to try,
And you shall hear the reason why:
Love has magic wings and flies –
It cannot be subdued by lies
Or malicious propaganda;
Now, dear children, please remember,
Love is free and won't keep still
But always travels where it will;
You know what the wise men say?
True love will always find a way!
When the daughter of the mayor
Fell in love, she was aware
That the source of her desire
Who had so set her heart afire
Was a despised, ill-treated Jew;
She never faltered, for she knew
That he was kind and beautiful;
She'd never be so dutiful
As to obey such hideous laws.
She loved him, they had every cause
To live as equals, now, forever,
She never would forsake him, never,
Though he, the good man that he was,
Pleaded: "Leave me, dear, because

You must not risk your life for me,
I know that I am all unworthy.
And danger lurks on every side,
If someone sees us – woe betide."
"No!" she cried, "your love is priceless,
I will not let you go, unless
Proud death decides to take me first –
So let my father do his worst."
They met within the green-domed church
In deadly secret, for a search
Of even the most sacred places
Would punish mix of different races;
In the gloom, an oath was taken –
Neither one would be forsaken,
Though in her Heart she was afraid
That by her kin she'd been betrayed.
Then hark! The tramp of feet ascending
The steep hill; then, sweet Love lending
Wings, they hastened up the stair;
The men below them cursed, aware
Their prey was gone. But someone saw
The tell-tale sign of opened door;
With cry of triumph, in pursuit
He led the way. The tramp of boot
Came ever nearer, as they clung
Together. The church bell was rung –
To raise the alarm – a dreadful sound;
They scrambled higher from the ground,
The soldiers nearing all the time,
Until sheer terror made them climb
Onto the topmost pinnacle
Of the silvery, slippery steeple.
"Have faith in love," she whispered, "hold me tight."
They leapt into the darkness of the night.
But, children, did they fall down to their death?
Or were they carried safely, on the breath

Of Love's soft winds, high up among the stars
Far from hatred, prejudice and wars?
So tenderly he clasped her, held her breast,
I like to think they found a place of rest,
Somewhere on this earth. Here ends my story –
Like blind Love itself, it's wreathed in mystery…
Happy ever after? Ah, who knows?
Beloved children, it is for you to choose.

Chardin: The Governess, 1739

They both know that the time has finally come;
The door is open, departure imminent,
And then their lives will never be the same.
Her lips are closed, but her look is intent –
It speaks of love and sorrow, hope, concern –
Is he too young to venture forth, to leave?
She knows he is naïve, has much to learn,
But O, how badly she wants to believe
That he will find new courage, will survive
His new life, far from her fond, loving care.
Will he miss her? Yes! Or will he thrive
In newfound freedom, when she is not there?
Gently, she brushes his new tricorn hat,
Symbol of his masculinity;
She'll pass it to him – then, that will be that –
He'll go, and he – and she – will both be free,
Free of the years together, close confined
Within this humble, warm, enclosing place,
Learning, exploring, travelling in the mind,
Finding immensity in little space:
They'd visited old times, wandered strange lands,
But when the door shuts upon her alone
Balls of wool must occupy her hands,
And cold brown walls will mock her gold-red throne.
He looks down, away from the fateful door;
He cannot meet her gaze, admit affection,
Even to himself, never to her. The more
He wants to, the greater the restriction –

He is a man now, must be dignified,
Befitting his new buckles and pleated coat,
Impassive, strong. And yet inside
He trembles, cannot speak, his throat
Fills, despite the elegant lace frill
Choking his neck; he must not show feeling…
He stands, hands clasped, outwardly quite still,
Quelling his pounding heart, his reeling
Thoughts. Childish toys must be abandoned
Racquet, shuttle cock, the playing cards,
He must become what Father always wanted,
A master of others, a soldier, marching forward,
Without regret. He will take the hat silently,
Lift up his head and with determined stride,
No pausing or turning 'round to bid goodbye,
Go firmly forth to face the world outside.

Constable: Flatford Mill, 1816

The wide quietness of the scene, its sweet tranquillity,
A held breath, a moment out of time – it looks so still,
A shining land of lost content, forgotten serenity –
A quintessence of England, these flatlands of Flatford Mill:
They stand above all toil, all tears, all harsh industrial change,
A simple rural scene transformed, something rich and strange.
But nothing here is really still, inside the painted canvas –
The wind that shakes the clouds and makes the clustered elm leaves quiver
The solitary reaper with his scythe, the horse in harness,
Who pulls the heavy barge along the flowing, rippling river,
The sparkling water of the running, sunlit-dappled stream –
All move within the static frame, as in an impossible dream.
All I can feel is that it is so radiant, so beautiful,
This art that brings the past to life, that can transport me there,
That overcomes the bounds of time and place, a miracle;
I release my indrawn breath to breathe in constable's pure air –
And feel contentment deep within, and welling gratitude
To experience such connection in the bliss of solitude.

Lorenzo Costa: The Concert, C 1485

Paintings of angels, saints, the blessed virgin,
Christ on the cross – all this is what I find,
Turning the pages of the gallery guide –
Beautiful, holy, too sacred for me
To dare to fathom what is in the mind
Of such celestial beings; how could I begin
To imagine their experience, delve inside?
How could I presume to try? But then,
Intent on my search, I turn the page again
And my eye is caught by this painting –
A woman and two men absorbed in singing!
I can guess something of what they are feeling,
Because I know the sanctity of music.
I muse that the heavens, resounding with angelic
Song, let fall a cadence which came down to earth,
And took root here, grew flowers, leaves, gave birth
To terpsichorean forests of celestial worth.
They're singing together in polyphony –
The shape of each mouth shows a different note,
Holding the rhythm through the golden lute;
Not unison – their threads of tapestry,
Are weaving a new form of harmony,
Each singer following his or her own part –
Together they create a perfect union,
As they combine the joy of being separate
With the holy spirit of communion.
The sound they make springs from the human heart,
And from the human brain's fierce concentration,

Above all, from the influence of the soul
That fuses all these parts into one whole,
Just as all the voices interwoven
Forge a new language that remains unspoken.
Time is music's fundamental essence –
You must keep time – yet time cannot contain
The mysterious element of silence,
Within and far beyond the timebound frame
Which, even as it moves, merges with stillness.
Was it thus the shepherds heard the choir
Of the great multitude of the heavenly host?
As if entranced, they would have kept quite still,
Lion and wolf enraptured too, on that dark hill,
The age-old urge to tear and kill, now lost
In hearing music of such rich, strange power
That it brought peace on earth, good will
To all the men and beasts who heard it there.
Perhaps, then, I *was* caught by something holy
As I leafed through the pages, one by one;
The fifteenth century artists who seemed solely
Preoccupied with painting their religion,
God in his heaven, angels on the wing,
Found such divinity when mere mortals sing.

Walter Crane: The Horses of Neptune, 1910

Only an ancient god could wield such power,
Feel only glory in the raging terror
That he inflicts upon the helpless shore,
Battering, pounding, with the fearful roar
Of waves that shatter, shake for evermore,
For this is pure and elemental war.
Gladly he sees, in that rush toward the earth,
The horses hurtle onward to their death –
Feels ecstasy, as those brave warriors smash
On rock, and break, obedient to his lash,
Disintegrate, and breathe their final breath
Of agony, before the pulverising crash.
Not for them, the grandeur of the charge –
They dread the sea god's cries, his bitter scourge –
Already, they are blown foam in the surge,
Mere ripples drawn back by the tidal urge,
Their wild spirit broken and submerged,
And from the mess of bone, blood, muscle purged.
Already, too, another line is forming –
Obediently, a second wave is gathering,
The horses start to rear, their nostrils flaring,
Their wide white eyes dilated, helpless, staring;
Neptune, relentless, furious in his daring,
Stretches his arms in triumph overbearing.

Dali: The Hand Remorse, 1930

From a blue sky
A tortured mind
From lands beyond
What we understand
Or reason why,
Stretches the hand
There trail behind
Broken promises
Clenched silences
Shame unspoken
Deeply buried
Almost forgotten
Tightly guarded
Wounds break open
Blood seeps through
From far below
Figures emerge
From memory's verge
Tiny, half-known
On a darkling plain
In lengthening shadow
You are not alone
Perched on high
Above shifting sand
On the slippery coil
Of a double bass scroll,

You hear a sound
Echoing, hollow
A long-lost theme
Begins to play
A ground-sea swell
Darkens the day
A tolling bell
A shuddering dream
From a guilt-soaked life
The hand will reach
Parent and child
Pluck from the beach
Husband and wife
The sea will encroach
Waves foam wild
Storm clouds break
Lash the ground
Flood the sand
Till all are drowned
And from afar
Sweep winds of war
You cannot wake.

De Chirico: The Mystery and Melancholy of a Street, 1914

A shadow child, she runs from her own shadow
As she hurtles headlong from the night;
Full tilt, her arm outstretched, she bowls the wheel,
Indifferent to Fortune; she'll not follow
A set path – but, as all young creatures do,
She'll stir and open in the morning sunlight,
Moved, not by experience, but what she feels,
And what she knows instinctively is true.
She sees only the clear blue sky above,
The dazzle of white arches and their promise
Of undiscovered worlds to be explored,
Eager in her innocence, careless,
In her impulsive urge to play, to move;
The warm wind blows her hair, the banner streams,
The way ahead is paved with gold, it seems –
She rushes onward, all danger ignored.
We see the land of shadows loom beside her,
The enigmatic box, the opened cage
With iron-barred, empty interior,
From which, perhaps, some furious predator
Has been let loose to slake its hungry rage.
The wheels are rusted, are no longer turning,
But she runs past, heedless of any warning,
Nor can she see the shadow cast behind her.
But there, enormous, in the setting sun
Another shadowy being blocks her way,

Arm lifted in a gesture of strange greeting;
The staff has been laid down, and seems to say
That they are enemies – that they are one,
That Time also runs forward, life is fleeting,
And those huge arches open into nothing,
And from them, only nothingness can spring.

De Hooch: Woman and Child, 1665

So long as men can breathe or eyes can see
So long lives this, and this gives life to thee.
(William Shakespeare)

De Hooch creates one tiny, priceless moment
To move all those who have the eyes to see;
His daughter lives here, always, through his paint,
All the more poignant, for the tragedy
Of his children's so short lives. He
Died in a madhouse, grief destroyed his talent,
His mind, his hopes; he left this legacy,
He showed us through this picture what life meant:
The child's delight at her discovery,
Her halo of bright hair, heaven-sent,
Her mother's joy in her dear family,
A love beyond what could be said or dreamt,
But captured here, in this humble interior
Transcending bitter loss and death for ever.

Degas: Laundresses, 1884

Evening, dim light and still they must go on;
By this time, it is hard to stay awake –
Weariness in every limb and bone
And sinew – backs, necks, arms all ache
With the demands of the relentless work.
Now they carry the fresh fruits of their labour
Up the polished stairway, all three flights,
Deposit them outside the sacred chamber
Where my lady's Maid in black-white splendour,
So different from their drab blue and brown,
Will ready her mistress for a gaudy night.
Their sweat and toil has made a shimmering gown,
Each mark washed clean, each rumple, fold and crease
Smoothed over by the sheer weight of the press –
The press of straining muscles on the linen,
And on the slipperiness of silk and satin
And on the hard hot handle of the iron.
The Maid comes to the door to take the basket
And they peer through the open slit, wide-eyed:
Of course, mere laundresses may never enter,
Can only wonder what goes on inside:
The Maid will check to see that nothing's spoiled,
While my Lady scans her silver casket
To find the perfect jewel to put on;
Her maid will fasten it near her white bosom,
Cautious, lest the fabric should be torn
By the sharp bite of a diamond pin,
Chosen to complement her smooth white skin.

All must be perfect, nothing stained or soiled,
As she leans close to fasten the corsage –
Flowers newly picked and delicately coiled.
My Lady's ready to enter the ballroom,
Radiant as a shimmering mirage,
This night forever gleaming in her memory.
A glimpse of froth and foam of petticoat,
As she glides forward; weightless, she will float
Swanlike above the crush and press and sweat…
The words recall them from their reverie,
And they must make good use of their brief night,
Must sleep and dream, before the breaking light
Summons them up those three steep flights again
To gather up the crumpled bundles of pain:
Their task, to purify what has been spoiled
By remote dwellers of another world.

Dürer: Melencolia 1514

Between the conception and the creation
Falls the shadow (Eliot)

Things hang heavy
Weighted by gravity;
The putto and the dog exhausted sleep
While slumped Melencolia keeps
Baleful watch; her glaring eyes,
Fixed in a stupor, stare at nothingness;
Her frowning face, her weary sighs,
Express a dreary emptiness.
Her flightless wings are furled,
Shrunken, like the miniature cold stone world;
One hand is fisted, tensed, clenched tight,
The other hand rests idle, cannot write –
The pen and crown of laurel ridicule
Her hopes; a metal pincer, like a manacle,
Lies abandoned on the ground
Next to the jagged edge of wood
That the smoothing plane could not make good.
And everywhere around
Used nails lie useless, will not fit,
The sharply serried knife won't cut;
The fragile wooden strut
Is far too weak to bear
The architecture of her doomed conception,
The magic oozes from the square –
The numbers don't add up, give mere subtraction;

The ladder is too rickety to climb,
And leads nowhere,
The brass bell will not chime,
The shining scales hang empty
In jeering mockery,
While unforgiving time
Pours out dry desert sands with nothing here to show –
The shadow falls and glowers, dark and low.
Yet those huge geometric shapes can seem
Like mighty fragments of a wondrous dream,
Now broken
Except for one which has – almost – survived;
If it could be caught, revived,
The numb trance woken?
If a wind from far outside,
A wave from the distant doldrum sea,
Could stir the torpid thoughts inside
And fight the weight of gravity?
Her gaze is fixed still, but within
The mindscape shifts, begins to rise –
A monstrous, howling creature flies
Bearing a banner like a winged dragon,
With a fiery promise
That she will again begin,
That her unseeing gaze will focus
Now, dazzling sunrays brighten,
A rainbow spans the infinite horizon,
And she finds her truest self again.

Feininger: Schooner on the Baltic Sea, 1912

As idle as a painted ship
Upon a painted ocean
(Coleridge)

The swell, the swoop, the surge of sea untamed…
Turner caught this, transcending limitation
Of time, of paint, of geometric frame –
The wild seas' roar inside a silent room;
Feininger spurns the challenge of illusion,
Ignores the watery element's fluidity
Insists on the truth of paints' solidity!
This is no moment in a flux of motion
But motion turned to stillness' purity –
Truly *a painted ship upon a painted ocean.*
Grounded on a small, earthen hill
In some well-cultivated field of green,
Where we are given the impression
Of mankind's ordering, tidy hand –
Straight lines of crops, borders dividing the land –
The painted schooner rests quite still,
Despite the angled sails which no winds fill;
The ship casts no reflection,
Except perhaps a ghost in another dimension
Of paradox, impossibility.
The wide, squared sky is ordered too
With overlapping planes of light –

Although a fierier, airier element
Barely begins to stir, to creep
Over the melting waves of the green deep,
To question the merely static view –
A mottled, dappled substance,
Which draws into itself a shiver
Of the sails' brown, earthy colour
To give, at last, a sense of dissolution
And of a shining, unseen distance,
That hints at space, time, motion
Beyond the frozen foreground of the canvas.
This knife-edge, manmade imposition
Extends the designed features of the schooner
Into and upon the chaos of nature,
And offers this reflection:
Constructs of human eye and mind
Exploit the powers of wave and wind,
And conquer the wild chaos.
But see where the white curl of foam
Escapes the frame, disrupts the canvas' stillness –
Whispering of the fallacy of man's dominion
Over deep waters that were once his home.

Ford Maddox Brown: Work, 1863

It seems a high-Victorian celebration
Of social order: each in his rightful place –
Complacency, in almost every face
That represents this grand imperial nation.
We're shown solidity in the brick mansions,
Their fine proportions admired to this day,
Resting secure upon well-dug foundations
In the clean mire of russet English clay.
The artist asks us to pause and admire
Work, in all its cheerfulness and grace,
The bright spades wielded like weapons of war
Converted into tools of prosperous peace.
I love the redhead lad's delighted grin,
His pride that he is ready now to join
The company of honest labouring men
Who build with pride and such determination,
Muscular strength, commitment, expertise;
They take the centre of this moral picture,
While other ranks become a decorative frieze
To highlight their heroic, fine endeavour.
Through their exposed blue veins, there freely course
Blood, spirit of the most ancient degree –
The ancestry of 'landed' peasantry
Which gives new meaning to the phrase, *work force,*
In this industrialised society.
They wait their turn now, the nobility,
Top-hatted, seated on their grand high horse;
The ladies, wary of the burning sun,

Shelter beneath their parasols' protection
Avoid the stain of earth on crinoline,
Keep their purity of class and of complexion.
It seems that now some of the men can read –
The posters advertise free education –
So all the more important is the need
For tracts that show the way to a conversion:
St Paul was struck with light on the high road –
So may these men be, by God's grace bestowed.
The intellectuals watch approvingly –
Their faith and hope rest in the written word –
Pleased with their success, they do not see
What lies behind them, for their backs are turned;
They seem to be applauding the young girl,
Who's richly earned these gentlemen's approval
In taking on responsibility
For her small siblings, doing her very best
To teach them manners, waiting patiently
Until their busy father takes his rest
From his daily task of sweat and toil.
"A fine example of The Family –
Society in miniature, where all
Value the duties which they must fulfil."
As for the homeless, here in Hampstead's heart,
Slumped by the roadside, cold in the noon's sun,
Silent, patient, they must lie apart,
Pale-faced, huddled, sleeping tightly curled
In this the greatest city of the world;
Here, where free speech and peaceful demonstration
Are sanctioned for the imminent election,
They haunt the shadowy margins, lost, forgotten –
Though not by the artist. Look! The largest figure,
Shuffling towards us, limping and downtrodden,
Is for him a suffering fellow creature
Who does not share the new prosperity,
The wealth of this great nation's industry,

Fostered by the power of Democracy.
Even the little dogs are better cared for
Than the poor ragged, barefoot, flower-seller;
She is coming near but cannot meet our gaze,
Is probably *no better than she should be,*
But her poor, lonely misery betrays
And tears to shreds our fond complacency,
Our vital core of selfish self-sufficiency.

Fragonard: The Swing, 1767

Oh yes, she knows exactly what she's doing –
Her stockinged leg lifting the petticoats,
Her shoe tossed titillating in the air;
She loves the thrill of flying, rousing, wooing,
While the swing rises high, just above where
Her hidden lover admires her daring, gloats
At his luck, reaches out a suggestive arm,
As with raised finger the boy Cupid silences all alarm.
He knows exactly what he wants; won't dally,
Dressed for the occasion in his foppish style;
That evening, there will be an assignation,
In this same burgeoning garden; her folly
Is none of his concern; may she beguile
The foolish husband, for this night of passion.
Ah, to be young and fancy-free and bold,
To sip the sweetest honey, before the hot blood runs cold!
But *he* knows nothing of what's been agreed
Before his very eyes. He holds the ropes –
His wealth bought her and she is his possession;
He lets her play, keeping her on tight lead,
Obedient to her duties and his hopes
Of an heir to continue the succession.
The little dog barks to see such furtive fun
But goes unheeded; complacent, he will surely be undone.
But does she, after all, know anything
About men's nature? All things rise and fall;
Now she is on the top of the parabola,
Loving the thrill, the danger of the swing –

All men, she imagines, answer to her call.
But she is young and ignorant of algebra,
She does not heed society's strict equation
That only disgrace and shame result from such risqué flirtation.

Friedrich: Chalk Cliffs on Reügen (Faith, Hope and Charity), 1818

They have reached the limit of the land –
The three of them can travel now no more;
Below them, chalk cliffs tumble to the shore,
Impassable, impossible, precipitous,
Vast, jagged mountains of destructive ice,
Where it is difficult to keep your balance,
Dizzied by the abyss, you cannot stand.
One has sought a bush's thin protection,
So that he will not slither, slip and fall;
His arms are folded in calm contemplation
Of the ships' diminishing white sails,
Imagining their unknown destination
When they have crossed the unfathomable ocean;
The ships are leaving home, heading for the horizon,
Where they will be out of sight, will not return.
What might they find, across the distant globe?
This man remains upright. His name is Hope.
The second man lies prostrate on the grass,
His eyes are closed; alone, he cannot face
What must come next. His strong staff has no use
Now, as he sees the limit of his strength;
His body measures the pitiful, small length
Of the life span that's given to all things mortal;
One step forward would surely be fatal,
For he might plummet to an instant death.
And so he prays for help with gasping breath,

Knowing he will be answered. He is Faith.
The woman looks down, sees in her mind's eye
Those who had earlier tried to scale the cliff
Who in their frailty had come to grief,
Could not recover, could not reach the high
Pinnacle on which she sits, still whole.
She reaches to these lost ones, heart and soul
Eager to help them in their desperate plight;
She cherishes the weak who cannot fight,
Knowing that love heals. Her grace, her sympathy
Fly on heavenly wings. She is called Charity.
The winds rustle the leaves. Here, even here,
The trees still cling to the thin soil, grow tall,
Sheltering us from what we cannot bear,
Telling us something of mankind's conception:
Descendants from the Tree of the first fall,
And of the second Tree that brought redemption;
To this pious artist, God is beautiful.

Friedrich: The Stages of Life, 1835

The expanse of light above is golden, numinous,
The horizon ringed with purple cloud, mysterious,
Over sea and land there lies a hovering stillness;
Is this the time of evening or of dawn?
It seems to be a journey of return
The stately ships are slowly heading home –
But are the furthest ones moving towards heaven
Beyond the rim of the world, their end unknown?
The nearer ones are seeking a safe haven,
Though rock-strewn shores will meet them as they come.
Wind in the children's national flag blows strong –
Together they hold it proudly up, above
The edge of land which overlooks the cove;
The young man beckons the elder, to come among
The family and their exuberant, innocent play.
But he stands silent, leaning on his staff,
Immersed in thought; he has endured enough
Of pride, even of laughter, and now his long day
Is fading, like the darkening sky of evening –
He looks to the far-off dawn, to a new lightening.

Gainsborough: Mr and Mrs Andrews, C 1750

It seems to me to be about possession:
The master standing tall, stiffly at ease,
Happy to be the subject of inspection
Amidst his wealth of stately, full-leaved trees,
Cross-legged, casual, formal, without passion;
His hound brushes against his satin knees,
Gazing at him with an absorbed devotion –
This is his kingdom – and he holds the keys;
As yet un-cocked, the gun could soon spring open
His posture says, *I can do as I please.*
What do I make of his young wife's expression?
She does not fully meet the artist's gaze,
Glancing aside, as if in contemplation
Of something beyond her newly married days;
She sits erect, feet crossed, in self-possession,
Royally dressed. Unseen, the tight-laced stays
Inhibit freedom: she is in the height of fashion,
And seems, like him, to welcome homage, praise.
But does the tight-lipped face conceal a tension,
Imply a possible parting of the ways?
The golden lushness of the well-tilled land,
The cattle and sheep inside the new enclosure,
The sheaves of corn, deftly secured by hand –
This perfect scene seems to pre-empt exposure –
But is there something we don't understand?
Within this portrait of arranged composure –

The couple with their confidence, their bland
Complacency – there lies an odd enigma:
The painting is unfinished; the wedding band
Is missing from her unpainted, absent finger.
Behind the elegant couple, dark clouds gather,
The harvest must be secured before the rain
Comes down to mar the gifts of bounteous nature,
As a cold wind sweeps over hills and plain;
The hint of change in the calm, settled weather,
Shows that their summer may not come again,
That they may not stay so decorously together.
I sense a faint unease, a latent strain:
The artist hints that things don't last forever –
In this unfinished picture there is unexpected pain.

Gaugin: Rupe Rupe, 1899

Annihilating all that's made
To a green thought in a green shade. (Marvell)
Now the rider loosens the long reins –
This must be, at last, the place to stop,
To rest awhile; to let his tired horse crop
The fresh, sweet, shadowy grass,
To break his journey here, to let time cease,
Ignore the questioning of narrow lanes
That bend and turn and urge you ever on,
 Against your will,
And to forget what still has to be done.
For here, it seems, both time and place stand still.
There is no importunate, *ringed horizon*,
No *undiscovered country* that he must make known,
No sense, indeed, of distance,
Only a paradisal quintessence;
The world lies all around him, now, now, here –
He'll let the horse roam free, then he'll step down
And feel the cool earth under his bare feet
And feel the warm gold air bathe his bare skin
And breathe the fragrance sweet,
And enter a new Eden.
The three girls will turn to meet his eyes,
Three Graces, free from modesty or fear,
And give him richest gifts of fruit and flowers
And welcome him into their lovely garden,
And there will be a timeless pause,
Beyond all reason, question, cause.

The sleepy dog may stir, her pups may stray,
The horse may lift her head and neigh,
The visionary girls may vanish like a dream,
And the old world turn and turn again,
And he resume his quest.
But ever after, this will seem
A place of absolute peace and rest –
The world laid bare,
Where luxury is simplicity and where
Everything is always for the best.

Mark Gertler: The Merry-Go-Round, 1916

Hampstead Heath, under a dancing moon,
People make merry on a fairground ride,
Loving the thrill, the spin and whirl of motion –
Open-mouthed, they chortle with delight.
1916 – a world at war. How soon
Will it be over? The officers bestride
Their rearing charges. Ah, but they have no notion
What will become of them in this splintered night;
Their open mouths emit a howl of terror
They cannot dismount or leave the carousel –
The women too are drawn into the horror
And all are frozen under an evil spell.
Round and round gallops still each horse,
Around the circles of an endless hell;
Mechanical, they keep their deadly course,
To the grim tolling of the funeral bell.
Forged from metal, impervious as steel,
Unstoppable as any tight-wound clock,
They carry their cargo on a turning wheel
Of fortune, which no human can unlock.
Now the scene becomes a blasted heath
Where bombs fall down from a moonlit sky;
No solid ground here – darkness lies beneath,
For this is far beyond all reason why.

Giorgione: The Sunset, 1506

He can go no further:
Light thickens, lowers,
The sun sets on the far horizon,
Its last slanting rays
Bringing a soft, blurred haze,
Casting dusky shadows
Over the path he can no longer follow.
There will be no completion
For this failed pilgrim,
His impossible destination
Recedes into the deep blue
Only of his imagination
Where it lingers in his mind –
A domed, spired, city,
Far from where he has come from,
Far beyond his reach,
Which he will never find.
His staff lies useless on the ground –
There will be no more journeying,
Only the sense of failure, burning
In his soul's blocked pathways.
Desolate, he is not alone –
Slowly, he warms now to the gentle touch
Of his loyal companion,
Slowly, accepts the fellowship of pity
Which strives to heal the festering wound.
He has strayed from the old track,
Which he has left, perforce, behind.

Reluctantly, he turns his back,
Then, for the first time, looks around:
From within the murky lake
Unknown lifeforms are swimming
Towards him in the gloaming,
Mysterious, curious creatures
Rising from darkening waters,
Beaked, snouted, wide-eyed monsters
That he has never seen before.
From under the old stone bridge
That leads across the deep pool's surface,
Behind the towering rock ridge,
Slowly, cautiously, in the thrumming silence,
Emerges an old, tusked, water-dwelling boar –
And slowly the image of his childhood hero –
St George, bedecked in silver armour,
Mounted to engage in chivalrous war –
Whom he had long worshipped in his dreams,
In this dim twilight of new knowing, seems
A lost soul who never can abandon
A worn-out crusade, his shining vainglory
Fitting the moral of a children's story.
Before him lies a curious, harmless dragon,
Gentle, baffled by the martial show
From a boy's world that was his, long ago.
Still the landscape darkens
With new in-sight. And there, over there,
He makes out a silent figure in prayer
Kneeling within a stony cavern.
Is this to be his new way forward, then?
To leave the march of onward travel
To find the Holy Grail, the frail chapel
Where on some glittering golden pedestal
The secret of all life might lie?
He will rest by this quiet, unfathomable pool
In the fading light of evening

Under the shelter of a supple sapling –
Which, though rooted in thin, rocky soil,
Will in time to come, grow tall,
Its leafy branches spread against the sky;
And, like the saintly hermit, silent, still,
Renouncing all the sound and fury,
Understand there is no need to fill
His manhood's cup with glory.

Giorgione: The Tempest, C 1506

She looks out with a challenge in her eyes,
Stripped bare, she shows no fear but only courage;
She is determined to withstand outrage,
Nothing in this bleak landscape will surprise;
She will be strong, protecting her child from evil,
And travel onwards, facing what may come;
She has no sanctuary now, no sheltering home,
But only her indomitable will.
He leans on his staff, but not on guard,
With an air almost of nonchalance,
For his is no intimidating stance,
Despite the dangers which they have endured.
He turns towards her, for she is the source
Of all his being. Fashionably dressed,
Unruffled, he takes his momentary rest,
Before they must resume their perilous course.
Unseen behind them, lightning tears the sky,
This moment frozen, before the roar of thunder
Reaches their ears. Will they turn in wonder
To see the darkening clouds, the ghostly city,
From which they had fled? Some dread disease,
Perhaps, had driven them thence in haste
To cross the rickety bridge across the stream,
Their past life tenuous as remembered dream,
And all their former hopes now laid to waste.
And, had they turned to witness the next fork
Of lightning before the onset of the tempest
Disturb their longed-for, necessary rest,

Would they have glimpsed the vigilant white stork,
Once bringing sign of life, now of disaster?
And had they hurried toward the foliage,
Fleeing the storm's pitiless, pelting rage,
Seeking the scant protection of a shelter,
Then, would the snake have lashed to bite bare feet,
And mock the state of man's fragility,
His hopes vain, ending in futility,
Their courageous journey incomplete?
This moment of peace, after all they'd lost,
Stands forever imprinted on our mind,
Despite the looming threat of cold and wind –
A shared love that lasts, will not be tempest-tossed.

Gossaert: An Elderly Couple, C 1520

They accept old age with equanimity,
Seemingly rapt in private contemplation:
He looks upwards with determination,
Grasping the silver cane of office firmly,
Holding his splendid fur-lined gown with pride–
His searching gaze, his jutting chin imply
The strength of character that lies inside.
Pinned on his black cap, a badge of love
Shines in the light that pours down from above,
For he still craves her touch; they stand so close,
The centre of life beside him in that place.
She looks slightly downwards, her expression
Showing her calm, clear-eyed, patient acceptance
Of what time will bring in his progression;
Her white headdress reflects her radiance,
And withered skin around her neck belies
The joyous light of living that she feels.
In both, there is a moving dignity
Precious as youth's passionate intensity;
They stand there as a couple, bound together
By their long past, their shared experience,
Their reliance on, their cleaving to each other,
Both innocent of any variance
That ever would or could cast them asunder.
What does the future hold for them, they wonder:
Soon will come the time of loneliness
When one of them must leave; the ache of grief,
Bereft of that sweet light which always shone

Before death came and one must live on alone.
Their age would give the comfort of belief
That there would be a blessed reunion
And life eternal in a heavenly kingdom. Alas
That our own age denies that faith to us.

Goya: The Colossus, C 1808

They wake to the bulls' stampede
That shakes the heaving ground;
They wake to the galloping pound
Of nightmare stallions, freed
At last from human rule,
Shaking off their riders;
They wake to the pitiful sound
Of braying, heavy-laden mule,
Patient and still unaware
Of what lies waiting there.
And only then they turn their eyes
Upwards to the blackening skies –
And from the dark recess,
Out of the deep abyss
Of human memories
Springs the dread word – Colossus:
And he? He does not even notice
The frantic panic that he has let loose;
He wakes to sunlight in his eyes,
The winds' soft caress;
He yawns, nonchalant,
Sleepy, indifferent,
Shaking off the dregs of dreams;
He is moving his slow thighs,
Stretching his heavy arms
To meet the morning air;
He does not hear
The panic-stricken screams,

The fearful cries,
The terrified alarm;
He has no understanding, no, nor care,
For an inferior species;
Indeed, he is oblivious to these
Miniscule figurines who swarm
Unseen under his feet and can do him no harm.
Is he some hell or heaven-sent curse,
This alien creature, this Colossus?
He comes from the deep
Of oceanic, underwater sleep –
From our unbound unconscious:
Not a doom-laden, wakened Kraken
Nor fierce, fire-breathing dragon,
No vengeful serpent coiled,
Come to our sinful world,
No cloven-hoofed, horned devil –
Black goat of monstrous evil,
Ready to wreak perdition.
With a gasp of recognition
We meet our own creation –
The horror is that he is human,
The horror is that he is one of us.

Goya: The Third of May, 1808

His inhuman courage,
Shown in the glare of the staring eye,
Its scorching outrage;
The tight-closed mouth defying death,
Stifling any cry for mercy –
That burning face
Seared on our memory;
His arms are stretched wide to embrace
Fate, while his fellows cower in fright,
Their hands shielding sound and sight
Of this darkest atrocity
On this darkest May night.
Their inhuman anonymity:
Heads lowered to conceal their shame,
Bayonets fixed, the riflemen take aim;
Each man avoids responsibility,
With military, cold efficiency,
Cowed by their target's passionate integrity,
Eyes narrowed, they cannot, they will not see
Him blaze a comet trail through history.

Graf Urs: Young Woman and Hanged Man, 1525
(The Twa Corbies)

I'll peck out his bonny blue eyes…

But she averts her eyes – she turns her head
To return a young admirer's gaze instead.

With one lock of his golden hair
We'll thick our nest when it grows bare…

But her new baby grows safely inside
And fills her swelling belly, feeds her pride;
Feathers are not for flying but to adorn her face,
She has no interest in death or in disgrace,
The cries of ominous ravens she ignores
Why be concerned with punishment and its cause?
She treads lightly on the sweet fresh grass,
Holding her woven basket, her costly pitcher of brass.

We'll peck the flesh from his white bones bare…

But she is young – whyever should she care?
The tree lends its branches for a scaffold
With equal indifference as for a nest –
It has been growing here for years untold
And knows that nothing's ever for the best,
For it has seen it all before –

Birth and death, peace and war –
It keeps its counsel – it is old and wise.

Grimshaw: Nightfall Down the Thames, 1880

If, after every tempest come such calms
May the winds blow till they have wakened death (Othello)
The wild waves whist (The Tempest)

In their longed-for rest lie the tall ships;
Only the gentle lapping of the river
Against the weather-beaten timber
Is faintest echo of the fearful thunder,
The roar and scream of Ocean's lash and whip;
Whist, now, the wild waves, whist…
Night falls peaceful here; while, rising into heaven,
The full moon hovers over the great dome,
Silvers the water; gone, the surge and foam,
The mountainous heights of windblown storm –
Now, just a stillness in this luminous haven;

Whist, now, the wild waves, whist…

The skeletal masts reach upwards to the sky,
Their rigging black against the soft green light,
The sails are stowed, the sailors no longer fight
To hold the course, defying the great gale's might,
Stopping their ears against its howling cry;

Whist, now, the wild waves, whist…

Here, Death has withdrawn and quietly sleeps,
Undisturbed inside the empty hold,
Not rearing up in glittering cliffs ice-cold,
To rend and sink, while women, unconsoled,
Yearn for news and cannot choose but weep.

Whist, now, the wild waves whist…

Frans Hals: Portrait of a Young Man with a Skull, 1612

And youth is cruel and has no remorse
And smiles at situations which it cannot see... (Eliot)

My eye is caught by the ridiculous feather –
Jaunty, tactile, flippant –
Atop his stylish hat;
His right hand reaches out,
Ready to grasp mine;
Open, joyful, confident;
O but his pleated cape is fine!
He thinks he has it all; I wonder whether
He really knows what life is all about!
His eyes ignore my question, gaze into the future,
Where he will preen and strut,
Display his costly haute couture –
The world lies at his feet;
With open lips and eager, impatient smile
He hardly hears the grinning skull
Mumbling through broken teeth, *memento mori*
His strong left hand strangles its feeble breath,
He will not listen; in his youthful glory,
He snatches life, heedless of death.

Hockney David: Garrowby Hill
Yorkshire Wolds, 1998

The colours spring to life from memory –
A fantasy of youthfulness now gone,
When things were seen and felt more vividly:
That freedom in motion as you rolled along
The rolling hills and flatlands of the wold –
The world lay all before you, before you were old,
And then your heart would beat more rapidly
As you approached the Hill of Garrowby.
The road became a plunging mountain stream,
Which you swept down, leaning into each curve
Keeping your balance through each thrilling swerve,
And on into the landscape of a dream.
Not wild, this wold, as the name might suggest,
But crafted with a fine patchwork design,
Each field contained within a clear blue line,
But leading toward the undiscovered distance,
Where you must travel, into the blue silence,
And come to rest…
But then, the sheer joy of pure feeling,
Freely wheeling.

Hogarth: An Election Entertainment, 1754

Here we have the tipping point in paint,
The guttering light of any last restraint –
Most are teetering on the very border
Of drunken joy and unrestrained disorder
And through the fug and stench of this interior
The artist captures the picture of hysteria.
The upraised stool and mallet, flying brick
Promise more violence; one brandished stick
Has missed its mark, and two men have been wounded –
More, in the coming chaos, won't be bounded
By any last gasps of polite behaviour,
Already lost to the rip-roaring clamour;
Still the musicians play, although the ship is sinking,
For there is fun ahead – and much more drinking!
The busy boy concocts the magic potion
Which, after more unbridled, wild commotion,
May finally induce a somnolent stupor,
Stilling the shrieks, the sobs, the wild guffaw,
The imminent blows of the impending riot –
All will, as under a spell, be deadly quiet.
Meanwhile, the gorging on the succulent oyster
Already has undone the gluttonous mayor,
Who's bled by an unscrupulous, smiling barber,
Sensing a profit in his patient's pallor.
Opposite him, and also on the alert,
A family is fleecing the Candidate,

Counting on his need to find approval,
They do not see the practised, deft removal
Of his gold ring. Enduring the raunchy kiss
Of the old woman, he is going to miss,
While revelling in the glory of his name,
The setting of his curled white wig aflame!
His colleague sits behind, his pipe raised too –
But the two leering men belong to a criminal crew –
With drunken embrace, they capture his attention,
Exploiting the politician's base intention,
To profit from the excesses of election.
The stare of the pot-bellied dignit'ry
Sums up the folly of the whole crazy
Scene; we catch his eye, he is unaware
Of all that's going on around him there –
His wig's askew, he's deaf to repartee –
Yet how the artist captures the irony:
Loyalty and Liberty, the flags proclaim
But Whig or Royalist seem much the same
To voters bent on being entertained.
Hogarth has both relished and condemned
This great stage of fools. Parliamentary democracy,
Britain's great gift to the world, flounders in anarchy.

Hogarth: Marriage à la Mode 2
Tête-à-Tête, C 1745

I haven't slept one single wink
It was a night of jollity –
My old friends would never think
I'd queen it over the *quality*!
For all the titled ladies came
So eagerly to flatter me –
To be invited to my home
And envy all there was to see:
The silver on the mantelpiece
'My' ancestors upon the wall –
The shimmering beauty of my dress –
Such joy, when they all had to call
Me 'Lady', saying, 'If you please' –
I scarcely could myself restrain
From blurting out, "You're being fleeced,
I'm sure to win the game again!"
For I know every sharp-card ruse –
The jewel of my education –
They were too well-bred to refuse
Another round of Speculation,
Or Whist or Piquet or Backgammon –
And not one dared to speak their mind
To say out loud that I was common –
Let them take me as they find.
As for my spouse, well, I don't care
Wherever he sneaked out last night –

The brothel, fleapit, anywhere –
I *want* him gone, out of my sight!
The little dog has caught the scent
Of something hidden in his pocket –
I won't fret over where he went –
My door's secure and I can lock it.
Now my chamber is my own,
With sheets of finest silk and satin,
Where I can laud it all alone –
Or let a close acquaintance in!

Hopper: Nighthawks, 1942

This is a desolate city,
Its wide streets are empty,
The neon glare of electricity
Heightens the darkness outside,
As you peer furtively inside
With envy, curiosity,
At those behind the shielding glass;
Shivering, alone, you pass
Closed doorway, half-shut blind;
But as you make your lonely way
With no particular place to go,
The brightly lit, coloured tableau
Stirs something inside your mind –
A scene from a dumb show –
And somehow bids you stay.
Questions hang in the cold air:
What are they doing there?
What draws them here together,
What keeps them so apart?
The icy atmosphere
Echoes the freezing weather,
And, after all, you would rather
Walk alone with your breaking heart,
Because it seems those strangers
Seated before the slippery red bar
Look even lonelier than you are.
So, as you turn the corner,
The image makes you wonder…

The single man is truly on his own,
Hat covering his face, he's looking down –
You imagine his worried frown,
As you pause on the street:
His back slumped in defeat,
His tight grip on the drink,
Haunts you, makes you think
Of some insufferable disaster
That he, like you, must now endure –
Perhaps news of the remote war
Across the heaving Atlantic?
The girl averts her eyes, studies one hand,
The other one not daring quite to reach
And touch his; does he understand
Her silence, or is he too lost
In his own tangled maze of thought
So that the thing that he surely wants most
Cannot be uttered? What they sought,
Perhaps, in this bright sanctuary
Away from the dark, deserted city,
Something alluring, soft, romantic,
Will surely come to naught;
Is it that some deception
Obstructs a true confession,
Obscures their real intention?
The burnt-out end of cigarette
Clouds the surface, cutting off reflection –
No meeting of minds here – not yet,
Perhaps not ever. *Only connect* –
But there is no connection.
These hawks have dived, intent, but lost their prey
And there will be a parting of the ways.

Holman Hunt: The Scapegoat, 1855

Look well at this scene of desolation,
The salt dead sea, strewn with carcasses
The lowering hills of heat-struck rock, bare, barren,
Air become fire, terrible silences;
This is the lowest place upon the earth,
The nadir lurking in your imagination –
The terror of each anguished, gasping breath,
The sheer futility of hope or of redemption.
There is no more falling, this is the worst:
Abandoned, damned and forced to bear the blame
Of others' sins; not honoured but accurst,
Bearing alone the whole world's guilt and pain
So that you may escape the mark of Cain,
So that you are released from scorching shame
By scapegoat, victim, saviour, horn-ed devil,
Suffering servant, banishing your evil.
Dare you meet his bold, accusing stare?
See your reflection in his black pupil?
Freed from guilt by him, can you now bear
To bend and touch his thickly matted hide
And feel his poor heart labouring inside?

Kandinsky Composition 8, 1923

A raid on the inarticulate…

But what business has the poet
To seek to capture the abstract?
As when describing music,
The mind falters and misgives,
Even so, the painting lives
Beyond the intelligible word:

The soul should be stirred,

Kandinsky explains,
Not the dull brain –
Words are thoughts, anathema
To this visionary painter.
This, then, is a travesty
And I strive in vain –
This is no fit place or time
For the lure of rhyme;
A couplet or quatrain
Gets nowhere near the heart
Of this intricate, geometric art –
I shall try again…
Geometry is the ancient term
For measuring the earth –
There is intriguing correlation
Between the natural shape and form
Of living things and the 'ideal' pattern

Musicians, poets, artists would all force
On elusive chaos through creation,
Echoes of a Platonic source
Glimpsed in flowers, snowflakes, spirals,
Those haunting mathematic fractals,
As if the spirit of the world has breath;
Through their precious intuition
Do they sense a route to the divine?
I do not know. I shall try again…
Straight lines, impossible in everyday experience,
Thrust and impose, strong, vibrant, intense –
Rectangular angles know no compromise,
Divided into clear, opposing pairs,
The black and white of squares.
Behind the gridlocked certainty, there lies
Something unknown. Grey clouds drift in grey skies,
Their half-formed curves expressing incompletion,
Uncertainty, hope, promise; their position
At the bottom of the mysterious picture,
Where, uncluttered, they have room to grow,
Shows the latent power of each creature
With imagination but without the itch to know.
The perfect circles are painted in bright colour,
Glowing yellows, reds and blues; the wonder
Lies in the eclipse, black and opaque:
Darkness reveals the fire of the corona,
Its hidden, golden radiance
Perhaps a celestial presence
That may stir and wake?
Timeless, the two-dimensional spheres are spinning
Eternally, with no end or beginning,
The perpetual whirl of being born and dying,
Change, with all its possibilities –
The picture moves before my eyes
Embodying metamorphoses;
I shall keep trying…

Now, the triangles are uprearing, rocky mountains,
Now, they are pouring, falling water fountains
Pale blue, gold-green, white –
Containing and giving light,
The motion is upwards, downwards and diagonal,
Transcending sense and gravity,
Irrational…
In the centre lies the rigid point,
Secure from any flying arrow,
Its essence dense, impenetrable, narrow,
Where time has ceased or else is out of joint –
A cosmic singularity?
Here movement stops, music gives way to silence,
Darkness' essence…
But see where the gold triangle enters the turning sphere –
This, wrote the artist, *is why we were born, why we are here.*
Have my bald words destroyed,
Made void
Kandinsky's metaphysical intention?
Would he be annoyed
By such clumsy intervention?
The painting is *the thing itself*
So let me not impose myself
By using mere words' *messy imprecision* –
I leave the artist with his purity of vision.

Khnopff: An Abandoned City, 1904

Patiently, the sea
Waits across countless ages;
It won't be long at long last, before
It creeps, in imperceptible, slow stages,
Over the undefended shore,
To reclaim its majesty.
Quietly, it broods;
No wind stirs its face, as still
As some patient predator asleep,
Dreaming of victory, and the overwhelming thrill
Of conquest, when it rises from the deep
And drown all in floods.
The city is empty,
The marble plinth is bare,
The windows are shuttered, blind;
The men and women who roamed that cobbled square,
Hold only in the caverns of the mind,
What they used to be.
Now sky and sea
Are pallid fog which merge;
The sun is hidden, nothing disturbs the silence
Except the gentle whispering of waves lapping the verge,
Unnoticed heralds of immense,
Unstoppable calamity.
Few have the will,
To fight the unrelenting ocean,
Fire cannon, brandish deadly swords and spears –
A hopeless, doomed intervention;

Works of many centuries
Must crumble, fall.
And what strange fish,
Swimming along the sea-green floor,
Will marvel at the ruins, its wide mouth agape
That its world of water had the power
To drown the city's alien shape,
Extinguish the bright fire
Of human wish?

Leonardo: Self-Portrait in Red Chalk (Aged About 60), 1510

He studies his face in the glass,
Even as he looks out at us;
And yet in neither case
Does he *quite* meet the other's gaze.
Those penetrating eyes look far within,
Refusing to be drawn
Into revealing the great mystery
Of his unparalleled mastery.
There is a grave solemnity
In the worn, aging face –
Seen in his lips, closed tight,
His overhanging brows,
The folds of the worn skin,
The bare, high forehead
Barely concealing the skull,
Acknowledging the coming night;
Yet such life in the beard
A river flooding full,
Moving, still.
For he had studied movement all his life:
Eddies, swirls, cascades, how water flows,
How the horse rears up in the midst of strife.
Birds' flight, man's flight to come,
Gauzy-winged dragonflies –
The dance of the Vitruvian man,
The baby's growth inside the womb,

Children and animals in play –
Such joy in motion will, he knows,
Defy the darkening of the day;
He draws in red chalk, using his left hand –
His right one now is partly paralysed –
And he, of all men, understands
That his art must and will survive,
Despite the ravages of time,
The imminent stillness of the tomb.

Limbourg Brothers: The Book of Hours – Sign of Cancer, C 1414

The heavens are telling the glory of God…

And so the noble Duke in his high state
Admires the wise, benevolent hand of fate,
The loveliness of God's created world
Which the bright stars in heaven have unfurled,
Making all things clear and in good order.
As for the lives beyond his high-walled border,
With its gleaming, patterned crenellation,
They too are part of God's divine creation;
And so and so, all manner of things is well.
The chiming of the church clock's sonorous bell,
Resounds throughout his land, from its high tower
And marks the passing of each golden hour,
While from the lofty steeple ring the peals
To summon all to worship; as he kneels
On his manorial pew, the great rose window
Illumining all around, drenching the shadow
With the glory of celestial light,
Stained reds, blues, greens defying night.
This is the time of Cancer – June, July,
When radiant blues suffuse the cloudless sky,
And when the golden rays of the great sun
Confirm that everything is being done
To nourish abundance in the fruitful earth:
When man works well with God, there is no dearth,

No plague nor famine, no frosts to destroy
The tender crops, for all is peace and joy,
And nothing has been left to fearful chance.
See how the reapers in a stately dance
Together with the lissom girls make hay
Throughout this sunlit, perfect, longest day.
By this he sees, when all fulfil their duty
There follow purity and peace and beauty.
Above, the stars are moving in majesty,
The Music of the Spheres in harmony,
Adam embraces Eve in innocent Eden,
Before the Tree of Knowledge brought its burden,
Redeemed, when second Adam brought relief
To those who follow the Way of true belief;
The chariot of the sun returns the sacred cross
To great Jerusalem, and so restores the loss;
The infidel is defeated, now the one God reigns
Just as the great Duke governs his domains.
All is ordained, and everything is meant:
The wonder of his works displays the firmament.

Lowry: Coming from the Mill, 1930

At first glance, factories dominate the scene,
Hard-edged, grey rectangles, towering tall,
From whose thrusting chimneys black smoke streams.
Not long ago, it was the tapering steeple
Which compelled the upward gaze of all
These decent, pious, humble Salford people
Who looked to heaven to find out what life means;
At first glance too, the stone church almost seems
A relic of lost time: dances on village greens,
Shepherds tending flocks on pleasant hills;
Now the men trudge tired, beaten, small
Under the weight of an exhausting day,
The grim demands of unforgiving mills
Which, of necessity, they must obey.
But look again! Each tiny matchstick figure
Is an individual who shines bright,
Confident before the changing future:
The lad who turns to greet the pair behind,
Two men absorbed in private conversation,
The hurrying girl with something on her mind,
The man in black who's lost in contemplation.
And now I see a changed reality
That shows the spirit, pride, humanity
Which lie within our shared human nature.
The street reflects the new electric light
As well as the dim gloaming of the day,
The red brick houses warmly welcome home
With open windows all those who have come

Back to their centre; a black cat is curled
An ever-hopeful dog eyes up a ball,
And in the park the little children play;
This is the past that made our present world –
The scene may be uplifting, after all.

Magritte: Pandora's Box, 1951

And each man fixed his eyes before his feet... (Eliot)

Punctual to the minute, always punctilious,
Modestly, appropriately dressed,
After eight hours working at the office
He has reached the river; now he crosses
The low bridge at his usual cautious pace;
A dim glow in the dull October sky
Makes him lift his head – and lo! he sees
Transfiguration in the evening breeze.
He stops. What has the sunset done?
Why is it he feels so strangely blessed?
How has this familiar, ordered town
Become a miracle of wonder? He cannot go on,
Some unknown spirit stirs inside him – why
Does the rose-red radiance move him so?
Beneath bared feet he feels the river flow,
Behind his shoulder, a white rose is growing,
And now he knows there is no final knowing –
He is suffused by mystery; below,
The cobbled stony road becomes an Eden
Where roses without thorns adorn the garden –
Ah! but where the serpent with forked tongue,
And the soft sirens with seductive song
Lead him into temptation. Now the aura
Fades as darkness settles, and is gone.
His black coat merges with the night; he moves on,
The box unopened. No, he is no Pandora

Nor was meant to be. He adjusts his hat,
Crosses the bridge, goes home – and that is that.

Magritte: The Lost Jockey, 1926

Furiously, the jockey whips
The tormented horse,
Lashes it to hold its course,
For nothing must impede the chase;
The sharp bit tears its lips
Its straining body heaves,
Gasping at every breath,
As mane and tail are swept
Upon the windless wind
Of the whole world's stage,
This exposed, bare place:
Curtains, half drawn back, reveal
Far, far less than they conceal –
Secrets dark, well kept
Inside the troubled mind.
Is he the hunter or the prey,
Hero or villain of the play
Which he can never leave,
Whose end is dusty death?
Nothing can help, nothing assuage
The jockey's wrath, his mad desire
To escape pursuing shadows,
Or catch what he follows.
With lowered head, he sees
Nothing of what lies before,
His cap's drawn down, he cannot hear
The music of the trees;
Motionless, he is confined

In webs of formulated lines,
Frozen by an unnamed fear.
In vain, the horse's thunderous pound,
On the splintered, icy ground
Beside a vast blue ocean.
Flying as a man accursed,
Betrayed, cheated, double-crossed,
Fleeing without motion
Inside a spellbound universe –
He holds the reins but he is lost.

The Lost Jockey, 1942

Now, the cold, windless air
Merges into endless snowbound plain;
Numberless new trees have grown,
Rank upon rank, stripped bare,
All their former music gone:
Perfectly formed geometry
Under a white, formless sky
Recedes into empty distance,
Holds only a senseless silence.
He is still and always only there,
Time and then time and time again.

The Lost Jockey, 1948

Flat rock scrubland, endless, barren, dry –
The black cave looms; horse and rider hurtle,
Powerless to leave its gaping mouth behind,
For it is always, always has been, there:
The dreaded, welcoming, dark portal,
Promise of rest, release and eery silence,
An enigmatic, terrifying menace.
In a familiar, alien, clouded sky,
Heavy in the overwhelming air
Hangs the huge, mysterious sphere,
Moon enclosed within a rayless sun –
No movement here of wax or wane
No rise or set; nothing to be done.
Helpless rage has brought him here,
Time out of mind, out of mind, again.

Manet: A Bar at the Folies Bèrgere, 1882

To prepare a face to meet the people that you meet…
Till human voices wake us and we drown (Eliot)

All is prepared, all ready,
Except the girl herself;
In this rare, quiet moment, she lets down her guard
And dives into green depths, under the facade
Of her ever-smiling service.
Her hands grip the marble shelf
Keeping her body steady,
She stands beside a precipice.
Her mind trembles, veers,
Shivers, as she holds back tears –
Such sorrow in that lovely, downcast face.
She has polished the glass bottles till they gleam –
In the glass bowl, golden lemons glow;
She knows she should shine, too, part of the show,
She knows how she must seem
To this louche crowd sophisticated, arrogant,
Who note the line of corsage, breast and pendant,
The delicate white foam of lace,
Pearls on her tight black dress.
She is dressed for the occasion,
Dressed to attract attention.
Behind her back we see reflected
The heavy crystal chandeliers,
The smirks and leers
Of tall top-hatted cavaliers,

So very well connected,
Never quite saying what they mean,
Wanting to be noticed, to be seen.
But this is what she longs for too –
Truly to be seen, to meet a kind man's gaze
As he looks gently into her raised eyes,
And seeks to understand,
And lifts his un-gloved hand
To fold her unclenched fists in his. Dazed,
She shrinks from common view…
Now she swims slowly, over a crystal bed,
Where deep peace lies,
Where pearls light the ways
And seaweed garlands wreathe her head.
The rising sense of menace
Returns her to the surface –
She has been lost, has gone far down;
Now fades the gentle sound
Of mermaids singing,
Seashells softly ringing;
She only hears
Laughter, groans,
Loud braying in her pearl-decked ears…
Human voices wake her and she drowns.

Master Bertram: God Creating the Animals Late 14 Century Master Bertram Contemplates the Sixth Day of Creation

I do not paint the God I was taught to know –
Mighty Jehovah in His thunderous majesty,
Jealous, vengeful – the God of David's psalms,
Bringing the warring Philistines down low,
Tempting the woman with the Forbidden Tree;
No – I show mildness in his lifted arms
And delicate fingers, as, like a choirmaster
Creating Music, this divine composer
Directs His newly formed harmonious choir –
Music of the Spheres given to our world,
That we may share in His celestial fire,
And feel the radiant light of liquid gold!
But then I hear the noise these creatures make –
And, with that sound, I feel my own heart break:
The swan's mute gasp, the gorgeous peacock's screams,
The crab's dull rasping, the cock's raucous cries;
Dumb fish doomed to silence fill the streams,
Stags bellow, pigs grunt, bats squeak, donkeys bray –
While the haunting screech of hunting owl
Makes hideous the calm of the night skies;
Loudest, the poor lamb's bleat, the wolf's wild howl
Who quells with glaring eyes his whimpering prey.
Why are these brute noises so unlike the goldfinch song?

God is all good, all powerful, and yet something seems wrong
The beauty of his creatures' form, their elegance of shape
He could not, surely, have designed to hunt, kill or escape?
And yet the crab's cruel pincers and the deer's cutting antler,
Seem formed only for battle, necessary armour
Forged to hurt the helpless in deadly, pitiless strife –
Such violence to stain and mar this new-created life!
And so I show a sadness in God's face,
A sense, dare I confess, of frailty,
Humility, not glorious majesty
Here, even here, in this sacred place.
On this sixth day, He will design a man,
The heart, the essence of his divine plan,
Made in His image, with immortal soul –
Of all His works, the highest pinnacle,
Ruling the animals, His supreme creation –
Yet free, alas, alas, to choose salvation or damnation.

Matisse: The Dessert (Harmony in Red), 1908

Through the wide-open window
On the wind of a warm afternoon
Fresh air softly blows,
Sunlight flows,
To bless the room inside;
The sparkling, blossoming orchard,
The shining leaves of the vineyard
Enter quietly, settle on the table, and provide
The spheres and lines of fruit and flower, bread and wine,
A pattern of perfection which will soon
Be offered to all those who come to dine,
As a form of sacrament,
A gift of nourishment.
Meanwhile, the branches curl and spin in ecstasy,
The flowers leap from their pots to pirouette
In arabesques of whirl and symmetry,
Paying homage to the beauty
Of man and nature's harmony,
That all who see this will never forget
That this perfected moment
Is how it should always be.
The window is wide open, wooden-framed
Where an endless distance is contained –
A work of art inside the whole picture,
While the magic of the artist's mirror
Turns branches into sinuous blue antlers,

The rich green of the land
Into a red radiance that glows;
The straight lines of the chairs, the barn beyond
Hold their still form, while all else shows
Shapeshifting, pulsing movement.
As for the humble maid servant,
Her eyes closed in prayer, her head bent,
A still point at the heart of all this motion –
She tells us of devotion.

Millais: Autumn Leaves, 1856

O Death in Life the days that are no more. (Tennyson)

The sun sets over blue hills – it is gloaming –
Both gloom and glow inside our memory,
Where winged thoughts fly roaming,
Then roost in branching trees of reverie.
The banked fires of the past are smouldering still –
Faint wisps of smoke upon the Autumn sky –
With thoughts which rise and flame, until they fill
Our hearts to overflowing,
With thoughts that lie too deep for tears or hurt outcry:
In silence comes remembrance.
Our lost selves stir, they rise up from the past
And meet our gaze with pale, reproachful stare,
Or bid a sad retreat with face downcast,
Or turn their eyes away, unwilling to bear
The knowledge of what they have now become,
As if in accusation or in prayer,
Confessing what their lives have left undone.
The leaves that once were golden now have fallen,
The apple has been taken from the garden.

The long day wanes…

Our past becomes a funeral pyre
Which will briefly blaze with golden fire,
Burning, yearning, turning
Our small selves into soft ash and dust –

We fade, as all golden children must;
The burned leaves will renew and bud again
Shoots spring from the rich ground
But nothing of us shall remain –
Only a wisp of smoke without a sound.

Millet: Man Grafting a Tree, 1855

It is the end of winter – early spring,
A chill light, muted, soft,
The sun in the east still low,
New leaves on the trees barely unfurled –
Time to begin
The annual graft,
Before the new sap rises from below:
This is his kingdom, his whole world.
His ancestors have won the lengthy war
Against the wilderness, have toiled to clear
The scrub, the tangle,
Bracken, thistle, bramble –
Hard graft, each unrelenting year.
Now he has been given
The fruits of all their labour long ago,
For which they had so patiently striven
So that their unborn sons should know
The joyfulness and the security
Of earth's unfailing generosity.
Behind him, the old cottage
Whose thatch came from the land,
Its chimney made of local stone,
Its doors from ancient oak,
Fashioned by a craftsman's hand.
Within, were born
The fruits of centuries of marriage,
All leading onwards towards his own,
The slow, repeated rhythms of peasant folk.

Now he stands here, in complete absorption;
His hands gently holding the new life
Which he will, in his turn, nurture;
His child, his loving wife,
Have come to see, in homage to his skill,
In wonder that just here, there will
For all their future
Come forth a strange new variation
Of the fruit tree; his Godlike creation
Sprung from the blessed trinity
Of child, man, woman,
And from love's immensity.

Monet: Autumn Effect at Argenteuil, 1873

Everything dissolving, shimmering, melting –
Air into water, sunlight into wind;
All is softness, rippling, trembling, lilting;
The river also flows inside the mind,
Giving a sense of peaceful contemplation,
All things suspended, timeless, as in dreaming,
Hinting at quiet depths beneath. Reflection
Shows a new world beneath the surface-seeming,
Where water does not quench the fire of leaves,
But gives the fullness of rounded completion,
Reveals a twice-tall spire, as the trees
Reach upwards, downwards, in a rare cohesion
Of elements, shapes, textures; the little town
Hovers between the river and the sky,
White clouds above, blue water flowing down,
All framed, contained, within immensity.

Monet: A Field of Poppies, 1873

A warm wind of summer softly blows
Tall grasses, whispering leaves, an elegant ribbon,
A blue silk parasol, clouds in blue sky; it flows
Up the gentle slope, even while the rippling stream
Of poppies courses down in joyful dance:
A morning stroll in a fresh field in France,
Where green and red seem colours in a dream.
I blink and it is gone.
Winds of time disturb, shake and distort;
History's stream rises, swirls, cascades
Down the hill towards me; I am caught
Inside a nightmare image of vast fields
Where red poppies are trampled in black mud,
Where green grass withers, knowledge only yields
A swollen river of blood.
I am haunted by these shades.
I open my eyes…wait; slowly, I return
To that lost country, forty years before
The world became a hell where red flames burned
And cries fell on a cold, indifferent wind.
The child is there still, gathering her flowers,
Absorbed, as golden sunlight floods her mind,
And time is only present in these painted hours.
Here, there will be no war.

Monet: Path with Roses, Givenchy, 1902

Seeing a reproduction, on a thin paper page,
I am bewildered by thick swirls of formlessness:
White, gold, red, orange, purple, green and brown
Merge in one great, rearing wave which drowns
The overhanging arches of the trellis;
Light flickers in the dapples and the shadows….
Now I can see the soft earth path which follows
The tunnel beneath the turbulent ocean's surface
Leading me into a strange, mottled darkness,
Perhaps the blindness of his extreme old age.
He had to ask for help to identify
Colours that shone in his imagination,
Not on the palette; alone, he could not find
The paints to match the picture in his mind,
The means to bring to life his inspiration.
An artist who can barely see – he saw the irony –
But shunned self-pity; we see poignancy,
The courage to continue to the end,
To follow the tunnel to its final bend,
And with dying strength, to soar on high.

Monet: Rouen Cathedral, 1890s

He was driven to capture
The flickering play of light,
Time's onward passing,
Through each timeless picture;
To show how solid stone can melt,
Light upon light amassing,
Like molten rock in the hot fire of sun,
Or dim blue ice as cold evening draws on,
Or flickering pink flames of hazy dawn,
As the great rose of the West window
Slowly emerges from the shadow.
Each time his subject vanished in the night,
He stood defeated; once again, he felt
The impossibility of his great mission,
The dying of his vision.
But then at dawn, he took his brush again,
And mixed the paints onto another canvas,
Resumed his doomed work with new hopefulness,
With a pure, dedicated, holy madness,
Eager to pour forth all his troubled being
Into the painter's task of simply seeing.
He must have felt a strange affinity,
With stone masons and glaziers long past,
Who would not see completion of their work,
But yet still laboured in humility,
Before they went into the gentle dark,
Knowing that their monument would last,
And grow in beauty for all time to come –

Our Lady's sacred, everlasting home.
But when he heard the great bells toll
So mournfully for every funeral,
As each sad coffin passed through the stone portal,
He felt anew that he was merely mortal,
And thought his art was too;
We, who live in times unthinkable
To him, can through him share his visionary view,
And stand outside of our brief time to marvel
At his ever-changing and eternal
Rouen Cathedral.

Monet: The Water Lily Pond with Japanese Bridge, 1899

Air, light, water interwoven,
In this unearthly garden
Under a hovering heaven;
The arched bridge floats in air,
Weightless, tranquil,
Leading nowhere,
Two-dimensional,
Set against falling willows
Receding into shadows
In the green haze of distance;
The water almost completes the circle –
A broken reflection
On the pool's surface;
Above, the fathomless silence
Echoes unplumbed depths below.
Held breath, suspension,
Wind whispering in the trees,
Rippling the pale water lilies;
Soon, the unknown resolution
Glimpsed here, if anywhere,
Floating above the air.

Moreau Gustave: Oedipus and the Sphinx, 1864

The brute force of that fierce, implacable glare
Where pure malevolence
Confronts blind ignorance;
He knows nothing of his birth,
She knows everything – her impending death,
His hideous destiny,
His damned reward for answering the enigma,
The gods' outrageous anger,
Devoid of pity,
All contained within the seething air
Of that seductive and destructive stare.
His back is up against the wall,
She pins him there,
The only thing he knows
Is that a helpless baby goes
On four legs, as *he* never could at all –
Abandoned on the mountain, helpless, bound
By one tiny swollen foot to barren ground;
Nor could he walk tall under the crushing weight
Of his implacable fate –
This maimed warrior
Must lean on his long spear,
A staff, a prop, no weapon of war.
Nor will he, old, creep slowly with a stick,
Three-legg'd; self-blinded, he will hold the guiding hand
Of his child, as he's banished from the city

To wander desolate across the land.
In answering her riddle, he seals his own cursed destiny,
Unknowingly.
All his piety, his selfless bravery,
Are futile to resist the playful trick,
Defy the loaded odds
Of the outrageous gods.
Is there one instant of shocked recognition,
That they are alike, both victim
Of a tragic, terrible dictum
Sent from above,
Designed to bring perdition,
Despite all his fine deeds?
Is there a mute appeal, even an attraction,
Even love,
As they meet each other's eyes,
A magnetic force of opposition,
Before their mutual destruction?
He will return triumphant, doomed, to Thebes,
And she will not unfurl
Those mighty wings, but hurl
Her lion body into the abyss,
Where, waiting to gorge on that strange carcass,
Shadows of indignant eagles reel.
So ends the story of the gods' great injustice,
So ends the story of the Sphinx and Oedipus.

Moreau Gustave: The Travelling Poet, 1891

He has the lovely face of a woman
The muscled body of a man;
He is chameleon,
A non-entity
Without identity –
He enters into everything
To bring
New vision.
Behind, unstrung, lies his mute lyre;
He sits on a perilous precipice
By trees that rise tall but are bare, leafless;
Below him, the barren, deep abyss,
Where black clouds swirl and seethe,
Sulphurous – impossible to breathe,
Raging, volcanic fire.
The winged horse paws the rocky ground
Impatient, ready to fly,
To open its powerful wing
And take to the limitless air;
It feels the rays of the shining star
Descend from the dawning sky,
And illumine the poet, while all around
Gold air is pouring from afar
Driving the darkness away,
Light of a newly created day;
Now it waits patiently,
Understanding what will be:

The poet will rise, take up the lyre,
Mount its broad back – and sing!

Berthe Morisot: The Cradle, 1872

Suspended in your crib with only the thinnest gauze
To shield you from the world,
How sweet, how deep your sleep;
Here, surely, is no cause
To fret, to frown, to weep,
To let the rising tide
Of fear that swells inside
Flood, so that I can barely any longer
Sit here, motionless, passive and still.
No! I must needs be calm
For here, there is no danger,
Nothing, here, that can bring harm.
The soft white draperies are furled –
Petals protecting the flower's heart
From the screech owl who flies by night
And swoops to kill.
I have kept my watch, and now the light
Of dawn breaks through the flimsy curtain –
Inside the room it is so quiet,
And all is known, is certain;
Outside, the song of the first bird
Blesses my child…
But now the mighty city's sounds are heard:
Huge horses pass outside the window,
The dogs have been let loose, the wild
Of wolf, of war within them; hunters, they follow
Man into the manmade wilderness
Of tangled streets, and winding, narrow

Alleyways of shadow
And unfathomable menace.
The gauzy fabric cannot stem the fear
Of what the future holds for us –
My tired eyes fill with tears
That my poor, lace-trimmed arm,
My helpless hand that reaches out to hold you,
Clutch, cling, enfold you,
Cannot keep you from the threat of harm.
Soon you will wake, open your sweet eyes
And meet my loving gaze –
Then all the fragility of gauze,
All the world's weary, angry ways
Will fade and dim: there will be just this moment
Here, now, always, of absolute content.

Munch: Moonlight, 1893

Her face reflects the moon, expressionless,
Haunted, in the emptiness of night,
Taunted by the ambiguous moonlight
Which has transformed the dreadful palisade,
Through which she has at long last made
Her escape into darkness:
Now the posts seem stems of shining silver
Their cut heads like the frail flowers which quiver
Fearful, beneath the window's guillotine;
Her head too seems severed from her body –
She has renounced her old identity,
All that she once was, all that this might mean,
To take her faltering steps alone, at last:
She's turned her back on everything she's known,
On all who knew her; she can be alone
Facing the dark unknown without distress,
Facing the enigmatic, changing moon.
But who is the furtive figure hurrying past?
Her other face stares, faceless, at the window,
Where the full moon is caught, reduced,
Shrunken into a small, globed lamp inside,
Casting little light of hope or reason;
Her looming, anguished shadow
Is trapped by the cage bars, still tied
To the old life within, which she once used
To endure, until its endless imposition
Turned her small space into a dim-lit prison.
But in the garden here, a red flower burns,

And she knows in her heart that her heart yearns
To escape the isolation, black, dark-green:
Should she return? What would that mean?
She's turned her back on freedom now, confused,
Her shadow darkening the window pane,
So that she cannot see her former self again.
Should she choose to stay or to pass through the gate?
And who is the fleeing red figure who will no longer wait?

Munch: The Dead Mother and Child, C 1898

The only thing she can do is resist
With all her strength, with all her pitiful might
The knowledge which the nightmare glimpse insists
That she must face. No, she'll not let the sight
Of the beloved face, the soft arms that caress
And hold her, pierce her consciousness.
Her mother lives, she lives – as long as she
Shuts out the senses that would tell her no,
Refuse to be bludgeoned by reality,
Refuse to let the darkness grow
And take away her dream of what is there –
And so her haunted eyes must stare and stare
At nothing; she has had to turn around
And fix her gaze upon the empty air,
Cover her ears so she can't hear the sound
Of muffled weeping or, much worse, of silence;
She's turned her back on what she loves the most
Outstaring death, in desperate defiance
Of what he takes and of what she has lost…
No, no, not lost! Wait, wait a little while,
Until the grim mourners leave and close the door –
Then she will turn again to see the smile
That is and will be as it was before:
Radiant with love beyond all knowledge, warm;
If she commands it, there can be no harm,
Then, in that unreal room, all will be always calm.

Nash: Dead Sea, 1940

How has our species' long yearning for flight
Become this mass of twisted metal carnage?
Icarus flew too near the burning sun
But his was a tale of daring and ambition
Born of his father's great imagination,
His craftsmanship and dedicated skill.
Visions of shining, winged, god-like creatures
Roused the spirit deep within man's nature,
As he lifted his eyes up unto the hills,
And wondered what another world might mean.
Birds were Leonardo's inspiration,
Their feathered wings light, delicate, unfurled,
A model for his famous flying machine
That might release us from our earthbound world.
This world's at war: look upwards to the sky
And see what brutal battle has achieved –
The degradation of the dream of flight,
Resulting in this terrible outrage
Where bombs are loosed like demons in the night,
Wreaking unimaginable slaughter,
Flooding the world with tears of those who grieve:
These weapons of warfare were designed to kill.
Here is a Dead Sea in a desert plain
Where solid silver waves rear motionless,
Cold metal in the place of running water –
Which cannot move, or heal, console or wash
Nor earth nor heaven clean of this new stain.
Air has been polluted and bright fire

Which would have purified, now only burns
In the ghostly light of searching flares,
And from the droppings of these murderous planes.
In the leaden heaven, the old moon stares,
Half-blinded, waning gibbous, her wan beams
Lighting glinting depths of waking nightmares,
No longer the domain of gentle dreams
Where she once shone unchallenged and serene –
All this has gone now. There is no return
To that lost world of innocence, before
The air became an element of dread
And Dead Seas were tainted with spilled blood.
Yet still the white-winged sea birds soar.

Picasso: Girl Before a Mirror, 1932

She is beautiful, serene,
Made golden, full-faced by the sun
Which makes her smile, red lips parted,
A warm blush on her cheek,
That's rounded like the baby safe within,
Who grows protected
By the peace in that inviolate place.
Now she can look anyone in the face,
No longer needs to drift,
Restlessly to seek;
Night shadows lift,
Leaving her haloed in white light,
As she alights on red-gold shores;
She reaches out her arm to bring the other close
In a compassionate embrace:
Look at me, find me, she implores.
But the other one is still at sea:
Blue-green waves are threatening to flood
Her frail, sunken womb;
Inside her mind, a waning moon,
A falling leaf, a drop of blood,
Outcast, she dare not come home;
She shrinks from the attempt to clasp
And draw her close;
She cannot meet another's gaze –
Least of all her own –
So she peers sideways,
Furtively,

Her head on fire with tension,
Gaunt with imagined loss,
Wanting to be left alone.
Her lips open in a gasp,
An indrawn breath of apprehension,
Beyond compassionate consolation.
We are one, we are not separate!
I had chosen to be blind,
Wilfully unseeing,
But what I wanted most to be concealed,
You have faithfully revealed –
My mirror image: the dark being,
Hiding in my heart,
My dread shadow;
You are also a part
Of the child that will be born
Crying, torn
From both our depths in pain and sorrow.
Now your sun's golden rays
Penetrate the dark sea of my mind –
The waters break;
Her first cry will be a breath of air;
She will awake
To radiance, find
Our warm arms enclosing her,
Look up to meet our gaze
From our lap, where peacefully she lies;
Then we will look down to see
A miniature reflection –
Ourselves new-born in her new-opened eyes.
For there will always be
Not each of us alone but three –
In inseparable connection.

Picasso: Weeping Woman

You stare at her transfixed; she stares at nothing
With wide-open eyes that cannot see –
The blur of tears, the nameless agony
Within her soul, preventing
Anything, anyone, from setting her free
From the biting pain that scores,
Splinters her being,
Tears her frail skin
With primordial claws.
Her teeth tear at the cloth to stop the cry
Of horror that she tries to hold within;
Her white face, clawing fingers, her clenched chin
Cannot contain the ancient
Black, writhing serpent
That issues from her parted lips,
The evil of a great eclipse
Of all that once had shone
Now irrevocably gone.
The painting strikes us with a blow
That catches our breath, disrupts all equanimity,
Searing our seeing:
Here is stark truth laid bare before us,
Pitiless, wordless;
We do not know
What has befallen her to shatter her whole being –
She is an unforgettable, haunting presence
In a vast, howling silence.
This is indisputably great art

Forged from the fragments of a broken heart
Where tears cannot be blinked or wiped away
But pour eternally.

Piranesi: d' Invenzione stet
Plate 15, 1751

The soaring arches reach beyond the frame,
So that no destination can be found;
Here life crawls helpless, without hope or aim,
In this palace underneath the ground
Where captives are eternally confined.
The concept and creation of this prison
Come from the hidden regions of the mind,
Deeper than truth, darker than any reason,
Nightmare inventions of such cruelty –
Imagined, yet with roots in history –
Artist and Emperor combining to invent
Manifestation of utter torment,
And force acknowledgement of inhumanity.
Whose are the giant heads fixed in the stone,
Blank-eyed, staring, suffering, malign,
Both guards and prisoners of brute instinct,
As they hang helpless as a tethered lion?
The huge iron rings of some vast broken chain,
Whereby man and animal are linked,
Show their intent to dominate, restrain –
Yet, soldered through their mouths, they're rendered dumb,
Silent victims of excoriating pain
For which no possible help can ever come;
The agony's deep-etched in every feature,
Epitome of the ancient urge to torture.
Their gaze is fixed, and so they do not see

The narrow iron stairs which lead nowhere,
Where figures struggle upwards, endlessly –
Because there is no door into the light
No wind to stir the suffocating air,
Only tormenting structures of impossibility,
And shadows of blackest night.
Some few men pause and lean across the rails
Where the vertiginous, empty depths beneath
Mock their puny efforts to cheat death –
Above are granite blocks; their courage fails,
Bowed, broken, wretched, they return,
Lie slumped or lean against the cold, hard stone
Defeated, abject and always alone.
Here, Man's creation rivals Hades' gloom;
The architecture of a Roman palace
Distorted into twisted webs of malice,
Woven upon the Furious Sisters' loom.
The artist makes us face reality:
With opened eyes, we stare at our malignity.

Pompeii: Portrait of a Man and His Wife 79 AD
(Seen in 1979 at the Royal Academy of Arts Exhibition)

This picture celebrates a great success:
Proudly, he holds his scroll for all to see –
Through his own worth, he has achieved entrée
Into the administrative class –
He who was once an ordinary baker,
Is now a man of standing; his ambition
Together with his quiet determination
Mean that he can wear the Roman toga;
A citizen of Rome – the envy of the world –
Model of civilised propriety –
A householder – mark of stability –
An ordered life so seamlessly unfurled;
His quiet, intelligent gaze, his handsome face
Please with their seeming lack of ostentation,
We warm to him and he holds our attention
Across the vastness of both time and space.
We like the way he stands close to his wife –
Paying the artist to paint a double portrait;
For he loves her and she is at the heart
Of all that is so fine in their shared life.
He's asked her to display tablet and stylus,
So proud of her that she can read and write,
As so few women can; he loves the light

In her wide brown eyes – to him, she's peerless:
He loves her hair, the gentle coil of curls,
The way they fall upon her soft, wide brow,
More precious far in their sweet, rippling flow
Than his marriage gift of gleaming pearls.
If beauty truly is a joy for ever
Then this love from an age so long ago
Still shines above the truth that we all know,
Though they could not: they would be torn asunder.

Poussin: Dance to the Music of Time, C 1635

There are bubbles floating, airy, gleaming!
Blown by the reckless boy, they have no power
To change their course in life, though seeming
As free as wind; they dance in sunlit hour,
These perfect spheres of light – alas, in darkness
They cannot find their way, are blind and helpless,
And must fall. *Life's troubled bubble, broken*
Before Aurora, rose-fingered, has woken
The heavens with her flower-strewn pink dawn.
In carefree play the bubbles had been born,
In sudden violence they must die, torn,
Pierced by rough ground under a cold moon.
Grey-bearded, grey-haired, yet still in his prime,
Winged, seated, naked, wryly smiling, Time
Plays dance music! Why *do* we blithely dance
When subject to indifference, to each chance
Whim of the two-faced gods who do not care?
Under their dispassionate, stone stare,
Man bears injustice, sickness, loss of love,
Suffering unknown to golden ones above.
Why play dance music, as for a celebration,
When we must seethe in futile indignation,
Crying aloud in lonely desolation,
Or, at best, finding hopeless resignation?
And yet the leader of the dance is Pleasure,
She looks straight at us with inviting gaze,

In bejewelled crown, winsome she sways;
Ignoring the hourglass and its trickling sand,
She firmly grasps the cosseted white hand
Of Wealth. One sandalled foot raised high, she's lost
Inside the moment, with her long hair tossed
Over her naked shoulder, her breast bare,
Intent on rousing an admiring stare.
Carefree, seductively, she treads the measure,
For on *this* earth, she has laid up her treasure.
Her face is turned from the youth Industry,
Who, ambitious, wears the laurel of victory,
Sure that his pursuit will bring reward
In Time; for now, the hours of work are hard
And long, as each exhausting, tedious minute
Consumes his energy. His aim is secret:
To drop the hand of hateful Poverty
And leave the never-ending circle, free
Through strength from what he was born to be.
He will give his blood, sweat, toil and tears,
To count his bondage in short months and years,
He will not countenance mortality.
He dances heavy-footed, awkwardly.
Next in the circle comes plain Poverty;
She alone looks straight at the musician:
Time brings a chance to change the dance so she
Might be released from her wretched condition
In this harsh world. Pleading eyes and parted lips
Express her longing for such change, a wish
That she might find release from life's harsh whips
And scorns, that Time might heal her anguish.
Industry grasps her hands, holding her tight,
Not in embrace but to prevent her flight;
She reaches out to Wealth who scorns her company –
Time's sands will run dry before *she* will be free.
Wealth is complacent, her glance fixed above
Time's enigmatic face; she dances with delight

With all at her command – she can buy love,
Fame, comfort. Clouds of approaching night
Gather behind her head but she looks east,
Hearing only the seductive charm
Of the ever-circling melody; she's lost
All notion of an end, she will escape all harm.
She is in thrall to Pleasure who clasps her hand,
She shuns the clutch of timid Poverty;
The world obeys her confident command –
As long as she ignores reality:
The empty plinth which points her to her grave,
The fragile tree whose windblown leaves will fall;
Of all her riches, nothing can be saved,
And she will hear only the silence call.

Poussin: Et in Arcadia Ego, 1637

Even within the dales of Arcady,
The harsh truth – cold, stern, implacable:
Here lies the fact of our mortality –
The tomb hard-edged, four-square, intractable,
Asserts its inescapable reality;
Although it is locked now, impenetrable –
Within it lies a power no one can flee:
Death, who is everywhere, yet unimaginable:
For even as light illuminates the tomb,
Shadows obscure its meaning in the gathering gloom.
The crouching, kneeling shepherds are confused,
They point to something which had been unseen –
The sunlit, hard-etched words leave them bemused –
Who is this stranger 'I' – what does he mean?
Here they have played together, danced and sung
All their past lives, within a sweet, green garden,
Where nothing strange or frightening lurked among
The flowers, where they lived like little children.
Some horror, in this most innocent of places?
Perplexity is etched on their young faces.
The standing shepherd leans upon the tomb,
His staff provides a sense of easy balance,
His look is contemplative, quiet, calm,
With perhaps, it seems, an air of nonchalance
As he reaches out a careless arm.
He recognises that Death fills absence,
Bringing completion, peace, instead of harm,
Perhaps the means to end frightened pretence:

He ponders the implications, unmoved, stoic,
Rapt in meditation philosophic.
The shepherdess experiences no strain,
Although, compassionate, she understands
The fear that others feel, senses their pain,
And brings them comfort in her outstretched hand;
This is a new idea – that men need consolation –
For care for others springs from sympathy
Within a world of fear and desolation,
Through kindness from the dread of death set free.
When next they roam their undulating pasture
This wisdom will enrich their human nature:
Death destroys; yet its idea can save –
Save us from selfish pleasure, careless joy;
The perfect balance in this painting gave
A wise contrast; too much of sweet would cloy –
The artist painted rocks as well as grass,
Dark clouds, as well as white, in the blue sky,
A breeze that shows us that all things must pass,
That it is right to know that we must die.
These four, no longer innocent, will be
Wiser, and live in greater harmony.

Puvis de Chavannes: The Poor Fisherman, 1881

The grey seascape reflects the poor man's sorrow:
An ebbing tide carries his lone oar's shadow
And nothing stirs the sameness of the scene –
A wide expanse of estuary lies between
The low line of the distant hills beyond
And the brown mudflats of the bleak foreground.
His head is bent, his hands are clasped in prayer,
In vain; it seems no heavenly help is there –
The skies hang low and heavy, like the seas'
Emptiness. Once again, he'll haul the net
To find no fish, only his hard times' threat.
Yet, on these same mud flats his baby lies,
Wrapped in rich red gown,
Contented, dreaming eyes
Closed in sleep not desperation;
The woman bends down,
Kneeling, not in appeal to the mute, merciless skies
But to gather flowers which have grown
On this same barren shore.
Some miracle that she saw,
Some source of inspiration,
From watery depths, unfathomable hallows,
Compelled her to make a garland for her man
With white, gold flowers sprung from imagination;
She will do everything she can
To keep the life in him afloat,

Even while his humble wooden boat
Is grounded in the shallows.

Raeburn: The Reverend Robert Walker Skating on Duddingston Loch, 1795

Behold the Reverend Robert Walker –
A most distinguished Scottish preacher,
Well-known as a learned teacher –
Renowned, above all, as a skater!
The Reverend sports a stylish hat
To complement his smart black coat,
A contrast to the white cravat
Jauntily tied around his throat.
Much material for a sermon
Can be gleaned from his obsession,
Enlightening his congregation
So they may learn this solemn lesson:
"If you skate upon thin ice
Then you would be well advised
To ensure you're properly dressed
To meet your maker – just in case…
Who knows what hazards lie in wait?
For no one can escape his fate!
Seek to adopt a nonchalant gait,
Spreading evenly your weight.
Balance is what's most important
Don't plod like an elephant
But keep your bearing elegant
Even, dare I say, flamboyant!
You should look forward, not behind,
Lead with your nose and you will find

This will ensure an ordered mind
And set example to mankind.
Best to adopt an upright stance,
Leaving nothing to mere chance;
Embrace the rhythm of the dance,
Eyes ahead, no sideways glance,
Fold your arms, lift up your head,
Like a gentleman well-bred –
Glide lightly with a refined tread…
You'll be remembered when you're dead."

Odilon Redon: The Smiling Spider, 1881 A Cautionary Tale

Children, you must never venture
Near this odd ten-legged creature;
Do not trust a smiling spider
For he's a connoisseur of torture!
He's just waiting to beguile
With his welcoming, warm smile;
Beneath soft lips, sharp teeth are filed
Ready to chew a juicy child.
Spider, you look so appealing,
But what desires are you concealing?
What innocence will you be stealing?
What horrors are you revealing?
O how cute his baby face,
His *en pointe* balletic grace,
His bristles soft as fine-spun lace –
But beware his dark embrace…
Run, little children, run, run, run –
He's no plaything, he's not fun
And he has only just begun
His campaign to get you done.
A silly girlie called Georgina
Was attracted by this spinner;
He sang to her, in his high tenor
But his aim was to bewilder,
To lure her into sleepy trance,
To mesmerise her with his dance

All to create the perfect chance
To hold her tight– and then to pounce!
O yes, he is musical,
His dancing is incredible –
But his toothy bite is fatal
And young ones are most edible.
So, little children, keep away
From smiling spiders who will say
Anything to make you stay…
Listen! Or you'll rue the day!

Rembrandt: Self-Portrait with Two Circles, C 1665

Herewith the worth of *the examined life* –
He faces himself, his viewers and the truth
Which is his solemn mission to reveal:
The aging, battered face, the wrinkled skin,
The meagre moustache and double chin;
He's chosen to highlight the bulbous nose
In plain, direct, uncompromising pose.
But he is also ready to conceal:
His left eye is in shadow, and his mouth
Half-closed; well-lit, the right eye stares
With uncommitted yet searching expression –
Not a wry acceptance or confession,
But rather, as I meet his gaze, a challenge:
To expose, without excuses, all the damage
Of a difficult life – *'tis much he bears.*
He holds the simple tools of his profession –
The slender wooden brushes golden gleam,
Tilting firmly upwards in direction,
So that, as we look at them, it seems
That they emerge from darkness into light.
The painter's hands are almost hidden from sight,
Caught in the dark where fore and back-ground blend,
But the old head is framed with shining white,
A simple artist's cap becomes a crown,
A message of power that he is proud to send.
Two mysterious circles, deftly drawn

On the lightest shade of all that brown,
Extend beyond the containment of the frame,
Just as he knows that his art will extend,
Through this and all his portraits, far beyond
His fast-approaching death. He is *become a name*,
But knows that his life's work has worth beyond mere fame.

Renoir: At the Theatre – La Première Sortie, 1876

Her first time at the theatre! Absorbed,
She leans slightly forward, her lips parted,
There, on the edge of the high balcony,
Society's cream below her quite ignored;
Her gaze transfixed, her wide eyes only see
The passing traffic of the stage; full-hearted,
She feels each swoop and fall of tragedy;
Clutching the fresh flowers in her hand,
She wanders in an undiscovered land,
A traveller in an unexplored dimension,
Lost in passionate intensity.
Dressed for the occasion, she can't understand
The occasion's rules nor her father's intention –
That she's been put there simply to be seen,
Enticing prospect for some titled man
To feel entitled to catch her attention,
Approach her, once the tedious play is over,
Present himself to her as leading lover,
Audition her for an important role;
Of this whole subplot she is quite oblivious,
Rapt in heart and mind, her soaring soul
Filled with the grace of unselfconsciousness.
Yet all too soon, the thick curtain will fall
And hide her; she will learn to be an actress,
Obedient to her director's call,
With lines to say, and vital cues to follow,

Enclosed in a costumier's fine dress,
Now centre-stage, leaving the merciful shadow
For the bright limelight of acclaimed success.
Graciously, she will play to the gallery,
As her brief story hastens to its finale.

Renoir: Picking Flowers (In the Field), C 1890

Poised at the edge of childhood now, they gather
A posy of wild flowers; they are intent
Upon their task in this one timeless moment;
The patch of grass where they sit close together
Is their whole world – here, now, without a thought
Of what may come. The white hat, finely wrought,
Carelessly dropped behind, is unimportant.
The joy of making such a lovely shape,
Each flower chosen from the soft landscape,
Contributes to the harmony of wholeness;
The sharing of this unreflecting happiness
Is all they need to consecrate their closeness,
Is all that fills each calm, unthinking mind.
Around, tall grasses quiver in the wind,
Dappled in the light like flowing fountains,
Moving towards the unseen far horizon,
Down the small valley, up the little hill,
Past the farm and solitary church tower,
Then merge into the distant, clouded mountains.
The radiant heat of noon is nearly gone –
Unaware, the two girls stay there still,
Above, the branches reach out to the future,
The couple far below cast a small shadow,
As they walk the path towards tomorrow
That lies in wait for every living creature
When the bright day turns towards the west.

Now, the warm touch of the field's thick pelt
Upon a hand, each delicate white flower,
The slither and shine of silk around the waist,
Is all they want, and all they have is blest,
Untroubled by the passing of each hour –
This is the crowning joy of all that they have felt.

Rousseau: Tiger in a Tropical Storm, 1891

He is the jungle…his black-striped, gold fur
Perfectly blending with the yellow leaves
And golden grasses of his habitat,
While patterned branches of the swaying trees
Conceal the fearful form of this wild cat;
His prey see just a hazy, tawny blur
As he lurks there among the swaying shadows.
He is the rain: the deadly hail of arrows
That tear and rip apart the blackening skies
Resemble his fierce weaponry of war –
The sharp-fanged, piercing, open jaw
Each raking, devastating claw.
He is the merciless fury of the tempest
That shakes this wild, impenetrable forest:
Lightning flashes brighten his fierce eyes,
Which strike such terror as they glare
Across the violent, storm-tossed air,
While his low growl of rumbling thunder
Deepens to a roar, presaging murder.
He gathers power into a deadly coil –
A blaze of fire, then the bolt will fall –
But not yet; he waits, he keeps quite still –
Then leaps: the crack of bones inside his maw
The blood-red turbulent downpour
Mark his kill.

Rubens: Peace and War, 1630

With the milk of kindness, Peace,
A half-smile lighting her mild face,
Protects all childhood innocence,
So that we think her power will never cease
Within the charm-ed circle of her grace.
Here is softest gold,
Shimmering in pleat and fold
Of flowing silken drapes,
In dress and braided hair,
And in the cornucopia
Of globed apples, tumbling grapes,
And in the leopard's eyes and downy fur,
Where, compliant and grateful, down he lies,
And in the smiling satyr's sun-bronzed skin,
And the wary maenad's bowl, wherein
Lie gleaming chalices and pearls.
Of darker gold, the tambourine
Is lifted skyward to sound the alarm –
For now we must look upwards, as the storm
Of War swirls in the darkening skies;
Pent, swollen clouds, blown on a brutal wind,
Bring only horror, threat of violence,
As cold rains fall on helpless humankind;
The furies are unleashed upon the earth,
And scowling Mercury brings news of death,
Brandishing his snake-coiled caduceus;
A ghostly dragon, with a lashing tail
And gnashing scaly jaws has been let loose,

Beside a sharp-fanged, rearing cobra;
The God of War is clad in blackest armour,
The glint of warfare in his ruthless eye;
Against his might, the wisdom of Minerva
Cannot prevail – victory goes to the warrior
And it must always be the frail, the fragile
Who have to bear the brunt of every battle,
For in his rage, Mars will not heed their cry.
What hope is left, then, for the little children?
The circle of Peace, so radiant, so golden,
Can never withstand such terrible onslaught
And all its shining promises will come to naught.

Schiele: Sunflower, 1917

Ah Sun-flower! weary of time,
Who countest the steps of the Sun:
Seeking after that sweet golden clime
Where the travellers journey is done.
(Blake)

Here, the doomed fight
Against relentless time –
The darkening of day's
Fading, fragile light –
Thin shafts, no constant rays.
The exhaustion of the climb
The burden of each hour
Defying gravity's power
To find the steps of the sun,
The flight that leads to heaven.
The flower turns its head in vain,
Its single eye is blind,
So how can it now follow
The shimmering beams again
When lowering winter's shadow
Mocks the futile struggle
Of those that once grew tall?
Now the radiant petals,
Droop and wither, fall,
The fresh green leaves turn yellow,
Scattered in the wind.
No rising from the grave

Our long journey is done,
The world cannot be saved —
There is only a dying sun.

Schwabe: The Angel of Death, C 1898

Life Is Very Long (Eliot)

The longed-for vision has at last now come,
Born on the wise winter's icy blast,
In the place which long has been his home –
The burial ground where all ambitions past
Have died; as in a half-forgotten dream,
She points the way. The spade falls from his grasp,
No longer needed, for she bids him welcome,
Heart pounding, he looks up – she is here, at last!
Dressed in a green that is not of this earth,
Deeper than the snowdrop shoots, which spring
And shake their heads for joy of their rebirth,
She shelters him in her encircling wing,
Breaks through the branches that hold him beneath,
Frees him from the circle of life and death.

Seurat: La Grande Jette stet, 1884

As idle as a painted ship
upon a painted ocean... (Coleridge)

On this fashionable island, men are islands,
Separate, distanced – they all seem alone,
Immersed in their own worlds and strangely silenced,
Resembling heavy statues carved in stone
Rather than breathing beings. Here, an arm
Is raised, not in embrace but suffocation,
There, another wards off threat of harm;
Only the soldiers march in close-rank unison,
Predatory, seeking out their out-cast prey.
Hats, scarves, parasols cut communication,
As each impassive, silhouetted face
Is turned, not toward, but always down, away.
Rods, sticks and crooks are all imbued with menace:
What are the shadows doing on this sunlit day?
The darkened foreground, the thick elongations,
The irrational angles, echo the windless wind,
Which fills sails, blows grey smoke in all directions!
The elegant young cox seems not to mind
That the four slumped oarsmen bend in vain
To move the sculls through the unmoving river,
Its water heavy, solid. There is neither pain
Nor noise – the trumpet's lifted but not blown –
Nor motion – the poised girl, the butterfly,
The child, all stiffly balanced on their own,

One cloud hangs heavy in one glimpse of sky;
The coiled-tailed monkey's tight-leashed and kept close,
The collared dog's too fat to scrabble fast,
The fan lies idle on the darkened grass,
And over all, an odd spell has been cast:
Time's stopped, and the imprisoned figures stand
Like chessmen, helpless in a dour stale mate,
Frozen by an absent magician's wand –
All they can do is to stay still and wait…

Spencer: The Resurrection Cookham, 1924

They waken from their graves bathed in dawn light,
Wondering how they had found this heavenly place
After the recent conflict's deadly night;
They blink in the dazzle of sun and behold peace;
Or, still sleeping in profound, sweet rest
Lie quietly within an ivy-sheltered nest.
Slowly, some stumble out of their stone tombs,
Pausing awhile to take in the strange scene –
Strangely familiar too – they have come home! –
Though to a home transfigured as in a dream…
Wide-eyed, they raise their heads and look around:
White lilies, daisies spring up everywhere,
Wreathing the church porch, covering the ground
With their pure beauty, scenting the silent air.
Haloed by shining white memorial stones,
The spirits read the symbols of past existence
And feel the joy that they bequeath a sense
Of life beyond mere reliquaries of bones.
The overwhelming silence is now broken
With faint, remembered cries of present laughter,
With words half heard in the distance, being spoken
By living travellers upon time's river
Who journey up the Thames to find their future.
But in the churchyard, time has ceased to flow
Upstream or downstream in a clear direction –
There is only this epiphany to show
The mystery of resurrection.

Steenwyck stet: The Vanities of Human Life, C 1640

This is a painting of such rich fullness –
Radiant with the artist's fine-tuned art,
Creating movement through its very stillness:
The meticulous arrangement of each part
Mimics life's journey upwards into night;
Yet see the shaft of sunlight that streams down
Made vivid by the darkness on the right,
Highlighting all with warmest golden brown:
Music within the shaum and dancing flute,
The lovely roundness of soft-bellied lute.
Lovemaking's shown by the uptilted sword,
Its point unseen: it never dealt with death
Rather, with new-born life, a spirit lured
By love, enfolded in a silvery sheath;
Its silver handle rests on caressing cloth,
Soft as the petals of a rose flower bed,
Far from destructive rust and gnawing moth.
The skull is hollow – what it thought and said
Lives in the books, half-open and much used,
Wisdom of ages, gratefully perused,
Perhaps in the quiet solitude of night,
Lit by the golden lamp, a precious treasure,
Which rests upon a music manuscript,
Betokening intellectual, sensual pleasure!
Golden, too, the exotic curving spiral
Of what had never been mere empty shell –

The delicate tip, the rounded curves are beautiful,
And summon still the ocean's heave and swell;
Poised on the table's edge it signifies a balance,
As waves of sea and music fill the silence.
In opened lid, still moving, the chronometer,
Unbroken circle of eternity,
Tells the times of past, present and future,
Reflects the light, casts darkness shadowy;
The blind skull may not see it, but we can,
The painting is for all men to behold,
To ponder on the little state of man,
To feel this warmth, though each of us grows cold.
The largest object here is the poor, humble pitcher,
Brim-full with water which pours beyond this still-living picture.

Steinlen Théophilé Alexandre:
Gust of Wind and Pastoral Scene, 1905

Who just ran by so fast?
Could it have been he?
Too late now to see –
Too late to take notice;
The man has gone
Lost in the gloom
Of tortuous streets –
An echo of running feet,
Then silence,
And the cursed anonymity
Of the great city.
A chill gust of wind
Entered her mind,
An icy blast
Awakening an echo
Of sunlit fields
Too poignant to bear.
Her heart yields
To longing, hope, regret:
Had he noticed her?
What if they had met?
Had he run past her to escape?
She will never know.
The springing of vain hope
Is the bitterest sorrow;
She must not stand and wait

But how can she face tomorrow
Knowing that memories last?

Stubbs: Horse Attacked by a Lion, 1769

A roaring silence
A raging stillness
One bare instance
Rendered eternal
Unforgettable
Seared on the eye
In the mind
Epitome
Of animal kind
The bone-bare battle
For survival.
Here, through the artist's skill,
Beauty is inseparable from horror,
Courage is intertwined with terror,
Desperation transformed into wonder –
The beauty of that powerful, turned neck!
Eyes furious, glaring, gleaming
Nostrils flaring, mane streaming,
Pure white body soon to be defiled,
The undaunted spirit of the wild,
Which the ravening beast will kill.
The lion is mostly shadowed –
But lit by fire in his eyes;
Hungry, he has followed
His victim to the precipice,
Knowing the very place
Where his prey could run no more –
The horse's fleet power

Cut short, where the rocky floor,
Gives way to the void beneath.
Bravely, he turns to defend
His life from the pitiless predator.
We barely see the lion's face
Only the brute strength in his claws –
His gleaming teeth,
In this momentary, endless pause
Before the inevitable end.
The trees cling to the perilous rockface
Or grow tall, watered by the lake;
Sunlight on the sloping hillside,
Cloud patterns which the fresh winds make;
In this picturesque sublime, the grace
Of pure, uncultivated, elemental nature,
Will bear indifferent witness that one creature
Has killed, and that another one has died.

Tanning Dorothea: A Little Night Music, 1943

She climbs the steep stairs, clings
To the supporting banister;
Her way's impeded by a *thing* –
She can't give it a name
For in her nightmare
Nothing stays the same:
The old, familiar corridor
Of childhood, long ago,
Now a forbidding hotel floor
With closed, dark doors,
Apart from one
Which swings ajar and cries out, "Come!"
But she cannot go:
Seeing its opened slit of light,
Electric shockwaves of pure fright
Course through her body, lift her hair,
And she stands petrified, cold stone,
Ignorant, not knowing where
Past innocence has flown.
The *thing* enormous, stirs, devours
Her unravelling clothes,
Now streaked with blood;
Her cheeks flush red,
With an unstoppable dark flood
Of some new feeling – shame?
She doesn't know the name…

Once there was a pretty daisy, white,
Pink-tipped, smiling in sunlight,
Why has it so monstrous grown
Its day's eye spinning, turning
In dizzying circles, fiery, burning?
Its petals now are ripped and torn,
Its pointed leaves lie fallen,
It stains her white dress with its pollen,
Its tendrils reach far out to touch her,
Snakes on the blood red floor, they clutch her,
And rise, writhe, hiss;
She screams…
Her older sister shuts her eyes,
And in sweet remembrance sighs:
Her tender body open, bare,
Her trailing, golden hair
Matching the flower,
Her mouth pursed in a kiss;
She clasps her bright treasure,
Light, plucked from the sun,
And dreams
Of the new-found pleasure
She has newly won;
On her, a little night music
Has shed its magic.

Titian: Bacchus and Ariadne, 1523

Abandoned, lost, these rioters –
Men and maenads, goatish satyrs,
On his donkey slumped, Silenus –
Following the ecstatic Bacchus
Charioted by spotted cheetahs,
Under tumid clouds above,
Careering headlong through the grove,
Indifferent to thoughts of love;
Beneath their tread the baked earth quakes
Above their heads the tall trees shake
All are eager to partake,
With unbridled greed and mirth,
Of raw meat torn from slaughtered calf,
Triumphantly and boldly brandished
To entice, excite the ravished;
The infant satyr tugs its head
Wide-eyed at the trail of blood.
Entwined with deadly coiling meshes,
Laocoon's twisted body thrashes
To rid himself of vile sea-serpent.
No one helps him, all intent
On cruel, ritual merriment;
Clash the silver cymbals, pound
Dancing feet upon the ground,
Beat the rhythm, blow the horn,
Bark the dog and bring the wine –
Forget yourself in drum and thrum
Of mindless delirium.

A startled halt – a quiet, indrawn breath;
Now Bacchus walks on air not solid earth;
All sound, in one heart-stopping instance
Fades, recedes into the distance,
Under an enchanted silence;
And on remote, cloud-topped blue hills
And in the star-crowned vastness of blue sky
All is still…
He is lost in a new-found land,
Abandoned,
Made captive and set free –
This is his destiny.

Turner: Hannibal Crossing the Alps, 1812

It is a visual assault of noise –
The maddened elephants' shrill trumpeting
Lost in the wrath of tempest that destroys –
The great winds' furious roaring, buffeting;
The thunder of the approaching avalanche,
The boulders' deadly rumble from on high:
This is the nature gods' most frenzied dance
To elemental music of earth and sky.
It is a frozen tableau of sheer motion
Circles of hell around the hurricane's eye,
Tsunami of snow from an impossible ocean,
Men, beasts, rocks, land and sky
One swirl of violent confusion;
Huge, uprearing mountains seem to totter,
Shake, under the force of the collision
Between earth and air, fire and water.
The Sun is God, the dying artist said, but here
The sun is overwhelmed, it seems, eclipsed
By swarming clouds of terror and despair –
Of all its warmth and light and power, stripped.
Those soldiers born in a far desert land
Of burning heat, in icy fear now cower,
Yearn for long-lost, lone and level sands,
For they have entered into the heart of horror.
Below, they glimpse their peaceful destination,
But they have come intent only on war,
Fuelled by old grudge and high ambition.
I wonder – did their experience of awe

At nature's rage, inspire these men of Carthage,
Those that escaped the terrible maelstrom,
With a new sense of pity, not to ravage,
Pillage, burn, but to be merciful, to be human?

Turner: Norham Castle Sunrise, C 1845

A quiet haziness, a soft dawn glow –
A windless sky hangs over the calm scene,
The silent river scarcely seems to flow,
Lapping the patient cow – all is serene;
High upon a rocky blue-grey pinnacle,
Reminder of past territorial war,
Stand the ruins of a mighty castle –
But conflict, bloody slaughter are no more,
For in this early morning there is peace
As the first rays of sunlight cast their shadows,
Giving hope that violence may cease,
Become dim rumour, reflected in the shallows.
Inviolate in its beauty, this radiance will last
When all our little histories have passed.

Turner: Rain, Steam and Speed, the Great Western Railway, C 1844

It hurtles onward with impossible speed:
From where we stand, there can be no escape;
It leaves the insubstantial, dim landscape
Of ages past, exulting in its powers;
Time that once was measured in long hours –
Each season's turning, the slow growth of nature –
Is being swept away, for now we need
To travel ever forward, face the future;
The iron-clad black horse will not look back,
Its red eye blazing, fed by fiery furnace,
On a fixed course, a hard metallic track
Along the straight and narrow rails of progress;
The passengers, bewildered by the wind,
Greater than any gale that sweeps the skies,
Deafened by the engine's thundering roar,
Blinded by hot steam streaming in their eyes,
Can't see what lies beside them, nor behind,
Nor how this present threatens all before;
They can't make out the swiftly vanishing past –
The land is lost in rain, a tear-dimmed blur –
But understand that old ways cannot last.
Dim in the haze, the arches of white stone
Stand spectral, silent, like a haunting echo
From another world; yet, still, a lone
Rowing boat is drifting away in shadow,
A farmer slowly ploughs his field's long furrow,

Though plodding workhorses will soon be gone,
With ox and mule and many another creature
Who daily toiled so willingly in harness;
From mists of time, an improbable Greek chorus,
Recovered from the spell of ancient night,
Lift their bare arms in wonder at the sight,
Moved by foreboding of a tragedy,
Awestruck, as the Fury passes by
Still carrying its age-old nemesis:
For there – just there – in front of the wild monster,
Hidden within his shallow, earthen lair,
Oblivious to danger, the brown hare
Who spends the chilling rain-swept hours asleep,
In sudden shock is startled from his dream
Where he pursues his quaking prey; awoken
By a strange cry, he hears the fearful scream
Of a wild beast in pain, smells choking steam,
Feels the foundation of the whole world shaken,
Gathers his strength and makes a fatal leap…

Turner: Snowstorm at Sea, 1842

(As preparation for this painting, Turner asked the sailors to tie him to the mast in a wild storm; the ship was called Ariel)

Lashed to the mast,
The churning, labouring paddle wheel
Inaudible in the blast,
He pursued his visionary quest
To bare himself that he might feel
The numbing swirl
Of frozen snowfall on his skin,
The dip and buck of sea, the raging whirl;
That he might find
How the waves rose to drown the wind,
Make a huge eclipse of midday sun;
Deafened by the furious din
Of the seas' roar
That wished the state of the world undone
In furious war,
Blinded by the cataracts' pelting pour,
Half-drowned, he tasted God's sad, helpless tears
As they fell bitter-salt
For mankind's sin,
For all our grievous fault
Our coward fears;
Saw heaven's airy vault,
Fragmented in the seething ocean,
Peered into the depths of hell;
With every dizzying lurch

And heaving roll,
With every soaring, plunging motion,
As the wild waves rose and fell,
Undaunted, he pursued his search
For mankind's troubled soul.
Did the frightened seamen curse
Thinking all was lost,
When he bid the cold winds do their worst?
Tempest-tossed,
They must have prayed,
While he, quite unafraid,
His eye still, calm,
Endured, stayed there,
Seeking the eye of the storm.
Here was immortalised each element
Of water, fire and air,
Here, like the brave spirit *Ariel*,
The artist *flamed amazement*.

Uccello: The Battle of San Romano, 1432

This is a rousing scene of action, horror –
Except that the heart and senses are all cold;
No sound, no touch or smell, no restless motion –
All still, made beautiful in white and gold
That gleams, too, in the headdress of the warrior
Who surveys chaos, carnage, without emotion.
The wind that blows the banner is unreal,
For nothing else is stirred; armed figures fight
In helmeted anonymity; jewelled horses rear
As dancers in balletic pose; unearthly light
Catches their harness – their frozen prance and wheel
Highlight their shape; there is nothing to fear.
Like slanted sunrays, lances lift to heaven,
Echoed by golden trumpets' silent blast;
There is no clash of metal, galloping thunder –
But a great quiet, as if a spell were cast,
Leaving the viewer with a sense of wonder
At the form, the finely crafted pattern.
The dead soldier lies prone, just as he should,
For deadly hooves will never strike his flesh;
The distant soldiers play in miniature,
As if held fast in a fine golden mesh –
How graceful they are! There can be no blood,
No tears of grief in this perfected war.

Van Gogh: Wheatfield with Sower, 1888

Lightly he walks on waves of soil, upright,
Knowing that summer's harvest begins here –
His outstretched arm needs no conscious direction,
Swings to the ancient rhythm, a pulse beat,
Felt in his mind and heart.
The cornfield is ablaze with light,
The slanting rays' reflection
Shining on transfigured earth;
A crow descends from golden air,
For eager-eyed inspection,
While another pecks the ground
Claiming his fair share,
Until the glorious setting sun –
Reminder of night's daily death,
Light and dark's eternal round –
Sinks under the horizon,
Calls them home to roost.
But he has many acres left to sow,
Before the dusky blue of the twilight
At last gives way to utter darkness;
Many more furrows still to go
Until he leaves the field, to sleep;
He skims the undulating surface,
Spring in his step, for no seed will be lost.
So the faithful sower proudly keeps
His age-old promise.

Van Gogh: The Sower, 1888

The low, flat grounds stretch to infinity –
Darkness gathers: the gold, whirling sun,
Dissolves and dims, becomes an eery green,
Leaving no radiance on those far, flat fields,
And their daunting immensity.
Heavily, he treads the clay-clogged mud –
Will his work ever be done?
He has given his long life's blood
To nurture the earth's hidden gold –
Its shy, reluctant yields –
And now the night draws swiftly on
And he grows old,
The black seeds fall on the churned soil
From his clawed, aching hand,
His fingers, withered, numb;
He trembles, overcome with cold,
Grey, huddled, worn.
But this is his fathers' land
And he will not succumb!
With down-turned face, onward he toils.
Lo! How the tree rears up towards the heaven
Defiantly, despite its poor, lopped branch,
Its bent black trunk, that echoes his bent stance –
Behold, the first new leaves are born!
He sees anew just what he has been given:
A precious inheritance –
To work the land, to scatter the good seed and bring
New life to all in each year's radiant spring.

Van Gogh: Almond Blossom, February, 1890

Van Gogh painted this to give to his brother, immediately after receiving a letter from him, saying that his new baby boy was being named Vincent. Van Gogh's move to Provence had not resulted in any sales of his work, so he was feeling very low. He had always loved almond blossom. Apparently, the family were delighted with the gift and kept this painting long after the others had been sold.

Late March in England, blossom on the trees
In our back garden; each morning I stare
At the windblown, dancing petals, white,
Delicate against the soft grey air,
I see that a few hardy bumble bees,
Even this early in the turning year,
Fly from flower to flower; two blue tits alight,
Perch on the highest branches, sing
And sing for the coming of the spring.
February in the South of France,
A letter bringing news of a new birth;
He is far from home now, in Provence;
Elated, he sets out on the ancient path
Into an orchard of blossoming almond trees;
They have given the baby his own name –
A sign of their enduring faith in him,
Despite his failure. He stops, sees
Knotted branches, grey, twisted with age
From which spring blossoms dancing in the wind,
White, delicate as clouds in the blue sky,

Survivors of the furious winter's rage:
New life, change, as each year passes by:
The grey cloud lifts, dissolves within his mind.

Van Gogh: Les Alycamps (Autumn), 1888

One of several paintings Van Gogh made of this place; sarcophagi line the avenue and a Roman necropolis was discovered underground. It was a favourite haunt of lovers.

The poplars are on fire, gold rising into blue –
Avenue of radiance – yellow, orange, red;
Shed sparks fall from burning Autumn trees
Breeze-blown, Moses' miraculous bush,
Flushed, like the strolling lovers, with desire,
Fire amidst fire. The old sarcophagi
Lie with their quiet dead on either side,
Hide skeletons of lovers now long gone.
On crumbling relics, the latest young parade,
Made dimly conscious of their country's history:
Mystery of the past fades, life goes on anew:
Blue tombs, blue branches echo the heaven above,
Love in its splendour lives, for all time, everywhere.
There once lay a city of dead, under the ground,
Found by delving deep, now covered over:
Lovers of Roman conquest whisper from the grave:

Save our memory in your heart, do not forget –

Yet these elegant young lovers do not hear –
Fear of lost love, life, is dissolved in this gold light;
Night casts no shadow for they walk at noon;
Moons may wax and wane, but they are immortal,
Eternal, their fire inextinguishable.

Van Gogh: The Bedroom at Arles, C 1889

Everything is pleasing, and in perfect order,
Rich blues, browns, yellows and a touch of red,
So that the room seems fresh but also warm,
Vibrant but calm;
The well-positioned pillows on the bed,
The solid strength expressed by the black border
Around the simple wooden furniture,
Which stand against the walls, each in its place;
And over all, the radiant, golden light –
Everything just right –
The lack of clutter, the harmonious space –
All is well-cared for, familiar, secure.
This room in Arles contains such vivid presence,
As if we too could come and take our rest,
Open the half-closed window, breathe the air,
Sit on a cushioned chair –
Feel welcome in the home, feel blessed…
Yet the room also holds a haunting absence.
The faces on the wall seem lost, withdrawn, downcast,
Eyes stare at nothing, do not meet his gaze,
White streaks on blue evoke an icy river,
Floorboards creak and quiver,
Spectral footsteps draw him into a maze
Where paths are blocked by dead ends from the past.
What does the black-edged looking glass reflect?
The cloth becomes himself, a thin, pale being –
A man exiled from such calm sanctuary –
Solitary;

This portrait of himself he can't help seeing –
Under the smiling surface, something has been wrecked.

Van Gogh: The Potato Eaters, 1885

The dark interior is full of light –
Not only from the glass oil lamp, suspended
From the bare beams of the dusky ceiling,
But from the warmth of family here gathered
Around the wooden table, every dusty* face
Expressive, vibrant with unspoken feeling
Of gratitude; they own this little place,
Can share the warmth of their companionship –
Their humble meal becomes a sacrament*,
Something blessed and deeply intimate,
Which transforms the lowering grey gloom,
The bitter cold of the black winter night.
Now that the long day's work has finally ended.
Fragrant coffee fills each shining cup,
With well-drawn water boiled on iron hob,
Poured from a shining, precious brass heirloom,
Its rich, dark smell flooding the little room.
Potatoes, unearthed from the stubborn ground
With such determination and effort
Are lit with an unearthly light, reflect
The bright eyes of these humble peasants,
As they share the hard-won food around.
The little girl seems haloed, radiant,
As she awaits her turn obediently;
The wife observes her husband tenderly,
As he stares, rapt in thought, silent;
She knows that he would never let her down,
Would always sustain their child, their aged parents,

Give each one of them their daily bread,
For all depend upon his dedication.
His hands' leathery, calloused skin, stained brown
From long years spent tending the precious soil
Are weathered by the unrelenting toil
Of each day's stamp and tramp and tread,
As, rising with the dawn, he goes
Among the long fields of potato rows.
From deep within their hearts they feel this benison –
That they can rest together in communion:
This is their lot on earth, their full-filled resolution.

Van Gogh spoke of his decision to colour the peasants' faces in hues of 'dusty potatoes'.
* *He also spoke of the sense of a religious rite such as The Last Supper.*

Van Ruisdale: An Extensive Landscape with a Ruined Castle and a Village Church, C 1665

Flatlands reaching to the far horizon,
Woods and plains receding into distance,
A huge sky where tumbling clouds are blown,
The blues and greys reflected on the surface
Of the flowing river's slow meander
Around the gold stone castle's ruined tower;
White swans add beauty to the peaceful scene
Complementing foliage of dark green:
Everything in this painting is serene.
A shepherd and his collie rest from tending
Their grazing flock of quiet, contented sheep
Atop a rocky outcrop; the extensive view
Stretches over tree tops, never-ending:
The windmill's sails, the sheaves in tidy row,
The red-tiled village roofs perched just below –
Create a timeless moment for all of us to keep.
Strong winds sweep across the sky towards you
Storm-laden clouds will soon obscure the sun,
And then the winds of time with threatening blast
Will bring the thunderous roar of ancient cannon
And sweep you far away into the past.
Soldiers on watch have shouted the alarm,
For they have spotted movement in the shadows!
Over the plains, across the level pastures
March enemy armies, shattering the calm;

Now they must fight these alien marauders
Who come ablaze with lust for battle spoils,
Must scramble to their posts on the round tower,
Through narrow slits shoot down a rain of arrows
Upon the up-turned faces of the foe,
Or prime their iron armaments with powder –
And fire down from mighty fortress walls.
The storm has passed, the present time recovered:
Tranquillity, plenty, faith; the grey church spire
Reaches to the heavens; nothing is higher
In lowland Holland where the undiscovered
Country is no threat; God, Man and Nature
All live in gentle harmony together.
But what will happen after, in the future?
How may time deface this perfect picture?
What lurks within our fearful imagination?
Ivy has probed the crack, the rocky crevices
Of the old castle's yellow stone foundation,
And that quaint relic of our martial heritage
After long centuries of wear has fallen down.
The river has dwindled into a mere trickle,
The windmill's windswept sail no longer turns,
The wheatfields that were once so golden, fertile,
Lie under a smouldering sun that only burns.
The church is empty, there are no more uses
For an old faith which reason will deny –
There cannot be an immaterial soul,
And men must live by fact, not empty promises
Of an eternal life above an indifferent sky.
It stands erect, an ancient monument,
The bell still there, although it does not toll –
It might disturb the many tall-towered residents
Who rarely venture out, but look far down
To the small spire beneath; the dusty plain
Under a cloudless sky is parched and brown,
The hot air swarms with bytes of information,

Stored in clouds that will not bring them rain.
I return gladly to the artist's vision,
The eternal beauty of his present –
To rest a while within the land of lost content.

Velasquez: The Water Seller of Seville, C 1620

An early work, this one, before the painter
Moved to the royal court – his subject matter
Then, the Princess, the great King and Queen;
Now, he creates this lovely, humble scene,
Immortalising water,
Illuminating wisdom, in the face
Of the old man who seems to be at peace;
His inward stare, lined brow and gentle hands
Reveal how perfectly he understands
Water's blest grace.
For in his hands he holds the element
Which gives life to all things, is heaven-sent,
Translucent like the glass's shine and gleam,
The elixir of life, as in prophetic dream,
A holy sacrament.
Gently he holds the pot of earthenware –
We see that all his deepest thoughts lie there:
He ponders water's goodness and its power,
As, in his wanderings among the poor,
He offers care.
The boy's face is still, suffused with light
For he too senses the supernal might
That lies in the glass he holds with reverence;
He looks into the distance, with a sense
Of angelic flight.
Behind, the mysterious third one of this Trinity

Drinks his life's cup in shadow, and we see
A quiet satisfaction in his mind,
A fellowship with all of humankind,
Through water's purity.

Velasquez: Las Meninas, 1656

Most portraits have the look of people that are looked at –
Scrutinised by artists, admirers, subjects,
Set against symbols of power and wealth, so that
The painting, with its choice of opulent objects,
Is designed to intimidate and to impress;
But here, the artist is the significant figure:
His richly coloured palette, poised long-handled brush,
Fine clothes, intent stare, all assert a character
To be reckoned with! Even his splendid moustache
Proclaims pre-eminence, as he stands tall,
Well-lit, inside the cavernous dark hall.
And his ostensible subjects? Robbed of ostentation,
Their pallid faces peer at us, nervously,
Consigned to near oblivion in a mere reflection,
Which won't reflect their customary majesty.
A pious nun and priest barely emerge from shadow,
Her hand raised in a benediction no one sees –
Ignored, too, the courtier, who beckons us to follow –
Rendered as adjunct, part of the background frieze.
The intelligent Infanta sees through the King and Queen,
And by so doing, she takes centre stage;
With head erect, bright-eyed, she steals the scene,
More knowing than others many times her age.
She seems unmoving and unmoved, with regal presence –
Young, innocent, untried, yet perfectly composed
In paint, as in her uncanny confidence;
Enigmatic, her thoughts remain undisclosed.
No questions, though, as we survey her retinue:

The kneeling handmaid watching every turn
Of her fine charge; the other maid subservient, too,
Glancing at the Queen for her approval; the stern,
Resigned, unhappy stare of the dwarf; her hands
Nervously finger her costume, her glum expression
Accepts fate's injustice; she well understands
That she is there to signify ironic opposition:
Her plain looks, stature, even her dull black dress
Are contrasts, setting off the elegance, the grace
Of the Infanta Margarita, future Grand Empress
Who, unlike her poor, dour self, has a lovely face.
The dwarf reflects the mastiff, at her feet asleep,
About to be provoked by the young jesting boy,
Who torments her too and makes her weep
For her role as curiosity, intriguing toy.
We stare at the starers, somewhat uneasily,
For at first glance, it seems they look back at us,
But no. Only the master painter knows what they – we – see,
In this unique depiction of un-self-consciousness.
Finally, we return to his sardonic gaze,
Subverting portraiture, status, expectation –
This confident puppet master, who still plays
With our assumptions, demanding our reflection.

Vermeer: Lady Writing a Letter with Her Maid, 1670

Light falls through the window
Casting light on the women –
Faces and hands illumined,
Inner lives in shadow,
In this quiet Dutch interior
Where nothing is revealed
Beyond the simple acts
Of writing, waiting…
The maid's burning impatience
Must be held in, concealed
Before her mistress' absorption.
The answer of the enigma,
Making the picture make sense,
Lies in the mind of the viewer,
Who must follow his intuition
Beyond the simple, bare facts,
As he seeks to decipher
The puzzle the artist has set,
Each peering across the distance,
Shedding his own light:
The elegant Lady writes –
The humble servant waits:
The women are carefully posed
But the window of light is closed.
How I love the unravelling
Of what was designed to bemuse –

The eager chase of the clues,
The wondering pause...
Peering, delving, travelling
Inside inscrutable minds –
And the things that I think I find
Will not be the same as yours.
The old masterpiece on the wall
Set thousands of miles away
Portrays a discovery:
Here, a dim light falls
Through darkening shades
On stony ground
On Pharoah's naked daughter
Surrounded by her handmaids,
On the babe in the water
Who has by God's will been found!
Is there an echo here
Of what may be growing, there
In our Lady's silk-clad womb?
Has her time nearly come?
The richly patterned cloth
Seems to conceal the truth,
Obstructs our view.
Who is she writing to?
Where will the letter be sent?
Why has she discarded
A crumpled scrap of paper –
So that it cannot be read,
Must not be understood?
Why does she shield its content,
Her back turned away, body bent,
So that her handmaid won't know?
But the girl has her inner life too...
Her face is alight with delight
And her gaze is directed outside –
Does she too have a secret to hide?

So calm, this ordered interior,
Where scurrying time stands still
For a fraction of a second;
We will never know what fills
The hearts and the minds of the women
Held here, without a beginning
Or end, commonplace and sublime.
We stay in the dark; they outlast time.

Vermeer: The Artist's Studio, 1666

And so the neglected artist chooses History –
Clio, with trumpet of fame and weighty book;
Yet there lingers a feeling of unreality –
The young girl with her timid, downcast look
Hardly fits the picture; the laurel crown
With which he has started, doesn't suit her pose,
She should be gazing outward and not down,
This modest girl whom no one even knows;
Book and trumpet lie heavy in her soft hands,
The death mask frightens her; she doesn't understand.
O, but *he* does! Before his eyes, before ours too,
This moment is recorded for all time –
Is being created, now, here, even as we view
This historic scene. His dream of fame
Is still only a fragment in his mind,
But deep within, he knows he has a claim
To be among the greatest of his kind.
Thus he links the future with the past,
Sure in the knowledge that it is Art that lasts.
We only see his back, clad in outmoded fashion
Referencing his predecessors' genius;
It is not hubris but self-knowledge, passion
For his calling, that tells him he will surpass
Most others. He paints a glory of light and shade,
Geometric patterns, cloths like waterfalls,
An empty candelabra, for it is *he* who's made
The light to gleam as bright as orient pearls.

Warhol: Diptych, 1962

But thy eternal beauty shall not fade… **(Shakespeare)**

Fade far away, dissolve and die…
Wiped from memory,
A pure white silence,
A blessed shroud
A longed-for peace
After the furious scrawls
Blackening Palace walls
The screams and jeers
Of a maddened crows,
The menace
Of fantasy
That made her a non-entity,
Wanting all things to cease
To be swept down Niagara Falls,
Its waters' purity
The means to an eternity,
Of sweet oblivion.
But she has not gone:
Golden girl,
Yellow, blue, red
Replicated
Countless times over,
Celebrated
On the cover
Of a thousand magazines
And this one soft silk screen:

Wide-eyed, the dazzle of smile,
Open scarlet lips
Still and always will beguile.
Death will not take her in his grip
She, unlike hope, springs eternal.

Watteau: Journey to Cythera, 1717

The long day's drifting gently to its end,
The ship's silk sails are being slowly raised
Westerly, the sun glows palest gold –
The fading light a solemn warning sends
That this time has been stolen from the day's
Wheeling diurnal round, that night falls cold;
This precious isle, circled by restless sea
Of life's demands of duty, caution, care,
Lives in the dreaming mind, the throbbing heart
Of lovers, who only know that *it must be*:
Uncharted but discovered, the true part
Of what lies all around us, everywhere.
Putti fly free in an enchanted heaven,
Venus becomes flesh – she breathes, she is warm,
Withholding the arrows from her wayward son,
Protecting all who love from any harm –
No threat can come inside her sacred realm;
At her feet, unused, lies gleaming armour –
The wreath proclaims that *amor vincit omnia* –
Except not time itself. The light will soon be gone –
One yearning glance before the homeward journey
With no sure hope that they may come again,
Except in undimmed, lifelong memory.

Whistler: Nocturne in Black and Gold – The Falling Rocket, C 1872

All art aspires to the condition of music… (Walter Pater)

Man-created magic
Overwhelms sky
Ear, eye
Green depths of lake
Reflect billowing smoke
Trees descend black
A bass undercurrent
Gold-fall rises high
A shower of sparks
Earth-and-heaven-sent
The curving arcs
Of a little night music
Shadowy figures listen
To the brass glisten
Of rising, falling phrase
Patterned echoes
Shimmering haze
Violin tremolos
Wind-lit flame rose
White hot intense
Then an immense
Silence.

Wright: The Experiment with the Air Pump, 1768

I can't look – I can't breathe – my poor head is throbbing –
All the birds of the air are a' crying and a' sobbing…

*

Behold the latest modern contraption,
Fashioned from the finest wood and glass –
I ask of you your keenest concentration
To ascertain how long the bird can last.
When I release the valve, then make an observation
If you please; together we shall note
Evidence of inhalation in the creature's throat.
And we shall see with due precision how
Oxygen is needful to both high and low.
Sir, your chronometer is set? Start counting…now.

*

This is most ingenious – a fine experiment
With many an interesting technical implication;
Ours is an age of science, enlightenment,
Founded on scrupulous investigation.
Although we cannot see the air with our own eyes –
Yet, we still know the cause why the bird dies.
I wonder, of the four essential elements
Is the invisible air the most important?

*

Who killed the lovely cockatoo?
O Father, it was you…

*

But I can't see properly –
You're standing in my way;
I really want to know
Which way it will go –
Will it be life or death?
I really want to see
The bird's last breath.
I want to turn the handle
Of that pump contraption –
Does it work by suction?
The flickering candle
Also impedes my sight –
Wouldn't it be more logical
(If not quite so magical)
To do this in daylight?

*

The full moon shines, the clouds disperse –
Shall we slip out, while all are so intent
On seeing this confounded experiment?
I care not for the outcome – better or worse;
This is propitious time for you and me.
I am yours for ever – will you, my love, be mine?
All else is nothing worth, is mere moonshine –
Surely, in sober truth, you must agree?
The candlelight that shines on your dear face,
Renders you radiant, and so full of grace!
Come, let us leave this tedious place,

And in the moonlight, there we may embrace…

*

My dearest daughter,
Allay your fears,
Wipe your tears –
This is no senseless slaughter
But proof of man's superior nature
Whom God made Lord of every creature.

*

Who'll dig the grave? I said the owl –
This is wrong, it is cruel.

*

I am too young to understand;
My sister's cries
Trouble me,
Why does she hide her eyes?
What is it she won't see?
I will reach out my hand…

*

I must lower the cage if it lives
And raise it, should the bird perish;
I don't know which outcome gives
More pain. Why should it be
Shut in a cage if it survives?
I'll ask for mercy – cherish
The poor bird, then, secretly, let it free.

*

All things in heaven and earth must die:
The flickering candlelight will not last long,
Nature's joys, encompassing birdsong,
Are all ephemeral. I ponder why
God gave us free will from the tree of knowledge
If science only serves for man to prey
On innocent fellow creatures. This is an outrage.
The changing phases of the moon
Are symbols of impermanence. Soon
My time will come – an airless vacuum
Lies within us all. This little room
Does not exemplify man's cleverness,
But his existential loneliness.

*

I saw him die, said the fly
With my little eye.
Ah, but I cannot witness
Such distress.

Wyeth: Christina's World, 1948

What *is* it she has heard or sensed?
A sudden instinct of alarm
Wakes her with a jolt
From dark dreams of war;
She twists her head to peer
Into the near distance,
Then keeps quite still to hear,
Straining each nerve to listen.
What noiseless thunderbolt
Has disturbed the silence?
Only the whispering grass
Golden, wind-caressed,
Warm in the sunlight, glistens –
Nothing that might bring harm,
And yet the spurt of fear
That nothing is as it was.
What lies over the flat horizon
That rings the limits of her world?
What danger have the clouds unfurled
In an ominous white sky?
There is no reason why
Her skin should shrink and crawl
Her pulse quicken,
Her poor heart sink and fall
Her held breath thicken –
No cause, no cause at all –
The house stands solid, square,
Tall, in the summer air,

Lit with early evening light,
Fenced in, secure…
But what has happened there?
And what is that wheel track
That leads over the slope of the hill,
Out of her sight?
There is no going back
Nothing is as it was before
And Time stands still…